DAVID WELLER

Essential Classroom Management

Systems, strategies and skills that create communities

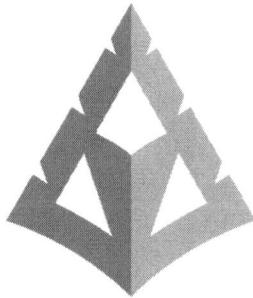

Visit the author's website: www.barefootteflteacher.com

First edition

ISBN: 979-8-71-448512-1

This book was professionally typeset on Reedsy.
Find out more at reedsy.com

To all educators striving to be better.

Contents

IX   Final Word

I

Getting Started

1

Introduction

In my first year of teaching, I had a class that gave me nightmares. They wouldn't listen, they wouldn't behave, and the only thing they learned was how to push my buttons. Can you believe I got butterflies in my stomach before every lesson? A class of 14-year-olds was driving me insane and nothing I tried worked.

Finally, after hours of reading behaviour management books, I got them to listen. After hours of observing colleagues, asking for help, and testing, I got them to behave. Hallelujah! Only now they listened, they behaved, but they didn't want to learn anything and sat there, bored and daydreaming.

I nearly quit teaching because of that class.

You can lead a horse to water, but you can't make it drink. You can make students behave, but you can't force them to learn. I'd been managing everything in the class but the relationships. I was treating students like objects to arrange, like furniture. I was teaching *at* them. This created a barrier to learning. They either didn't trust me, didn't like me, or didn't respect me (or all three!). No wonder they didn't engage with me or my lessons.

Classroom management is the art and science of preparing students to learn, and the essence of classroom management is relationship management. Learning happens when a student engages with, and thinks about, the lesson material. You can control a student's environment, but not what happens in their head. The better the relationship you have with your students, the more they trust you. The more they trust you, the more you can influence them to learn.

For newer teachers, as I was, classroom management seems to start with fixing unwanted behaviour. If you're having trouble with a particular class, then visit section 7, 'Managing Behavior' now. The techniques there will help you put a band-aid over the worst offences. The goal though, is to prevent bad behaviour ever happening.

I recommend working through this book in sequence. Each section builds on the one before. You'll learn to better manage the environment, yourself, your students and (hopefully) their learning. You'll arrive at the end of this journey with classroom management so polished that misbehaviour rarely occurs, if at all.

So use this book as a step-by-step guide. Work through one chapter at a time, trying, testing and seeing how it affects your lessons. Implement slowly and don't change too much at once. You'll avoid the stress of your brain melting with too much information. Your students will benefit from not being confused, which leads to more misbehaviour. Small changes, consistently applied, will transform your teaching.

Note: this book assumes that you've already planned your lesson, prepared your materials, and are ready to teach. If not (and you're a language teacher) then you can get a head start on how to plan by using my book 'Lesson Planning for Language Teachers'[1].

2

What is Classroom Management?

Classroom management refers to all the skills and techniques teachers use to support learning. There's no one right way to teach, so over the years teacher have developed *lots* of methods, to fit them and their students. Fortunately, all of these can be grouped into categories, and each is a section in this book. They are:

- Managing the environment
- Managing yourself
- Managing relationships
- Managing behaviour
- Managing engagement
- Managing activities
- Managing learning

Managing the environment means organising your physical or virtual teaching location. All students instinctively respond well to a clean, tidy, welcoming space.

Before you can manage others well, you need to manage yourself. Your spoken and body language, habits, mannerisms and personal routines are all aspects of self-management. You need to become aware of your habits before you can decide if you want to change them.

It's then time to focus on relationships in the classroom. This means more than the interpersonal dynamics between you and your students, it also includes the students' relationship with each other, attitude towards the teaching material, and parents' attitudes. Building those relationships will stop some misbehaviour, but we'll look at why misbehaviour occurs and what it takes to correct minor, serious, and consistent misbehaviour.

Once a class is behaving well, they need to be engaged. This means focusing their attention on something you choose, rather than talking to friends or daydreaming. We'll look at how to focus and maintain engagement. This engagement is then used to run successful activities. We'll look at ways of running an activity that flow smoothly, without giving students a chance to get distracted or lose focus.

Now, there's a high chance your students are learning. We still need to check this is true, and manage their learning so it can be as effective as possible.

These seven areas are broadly sequential, so I've put them into a hierarchy, and we'll look at them in this order. If you follow this sequence of actions and changes, you'll see a revolutionary change in your lessons, your students' behaviour and their learning outcomes (and you'll feel less stressed!)

7. Learning

6. Activities

5. Engagement

4. Behaviour

3. Relationships

2. Yourself

1. Environment

A hierarchy of classroom management

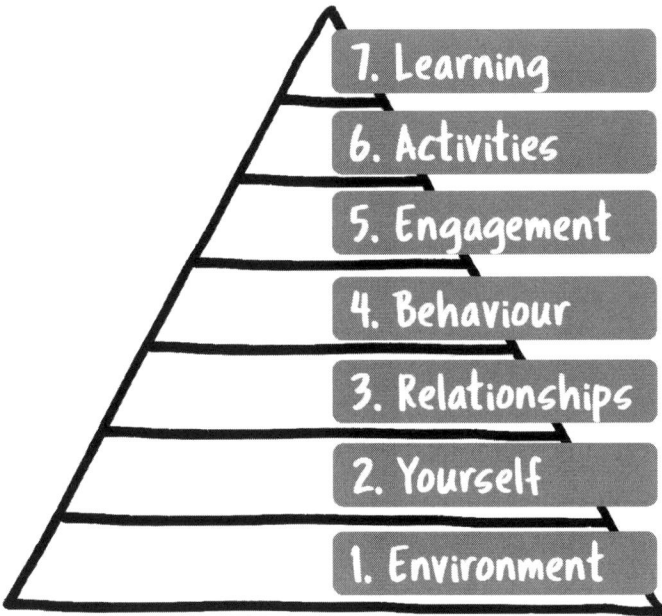

3

What It's Not

Classroom management is a lot of things, but there are four things it especially *isn't*. These four ideas are often included in teacher training courses, or passed down in staffrooms. Although they're persistent, don't be fooled. Believing will put a dent in your plans to master classroom management.

Myth #1: Noisy Class = No Learning

Some of the greatest learning moments happen in a noisy class. Sure, the teacher may have had a breakdown and the students are running riot. But assuming good classroom management, learning is likely flourishing. Learning can be (and often is) collaborative, which means learning can be loud. Learn to love it. Also note the reverse isn't always true—a silent class doesn't guarantee learning either. Silence can hide confusion, boredom, and daydreams. It's just harder to fake noisy engagement.

Myth #2: Classroom Management = Discipline

Newer teachers assume that discipline is the start and end of classroom management. You often hear new teachers talking about how to 'keep discipline'. Losing control of a class is probably their biggest fear. Effective behaviour management is about far more than discipline. As we'll see throughout, preventing unwanted behaviour is more effective than managing it. Avoid fires starting, rather than getting good at extinguishing them.

Myth #3: Classroom Management = Rewards and Punishments

Classroom management is more than rewards and punishments. Positive reinforcement is great for rewarding good behaviour, and you need a 'hier-archy of consequences' (see chapter 45) for more serious misbehaviour. If the only tool you have is a hammer, then everything looks like a nail, and you'll overuse these techniques. If well-behaved students are always praised, and naughty students always punished, then accusations of unfairness and favouritism will start.

Myth #4: Classroom Management = Entertaining Students

Some teachers appear to have success by keeping students entertained at all times (sometimes called 'edutainment'). By using humour and always playing games, they avoid misbehaviour. There are two issues—first, it's dubious how much learning happens if students don't get the chance to think. Second, over time your students will demand ever-more entertainment as they get bored with the current level, until they start to misbehave. This is known as hedonistic adaptation[2].

4

Aims

Classroom management has two aims[3]:

1. To create an environment for academic learning
2. To create an environment for socio-emotional learning

Academic learning is the content of the curriculum. Socio-emotional learning refers to growing emotionally and acquiring social skills. Create the conditions for both, and you give your students the best opportunity to succeed.

Academic Learning Environment

The Ideal Classroom

Socio-Emotional Learning Environment

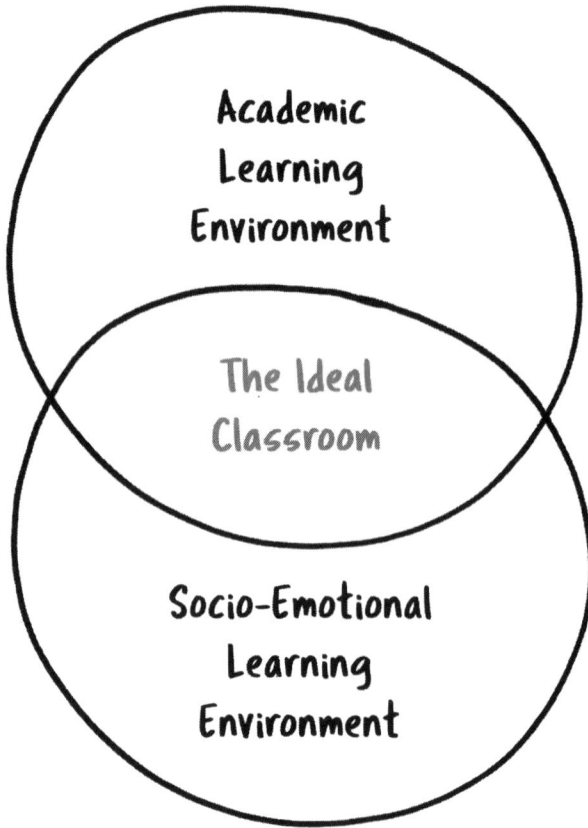

The two aims of classroom management

5

Benefits

Teaching is messy, and trying to get students to sit still, pay attention, behave, and focus... well, it doesn't happen by accident. You need classroom management skills.

Unluckily, teacher training courses suck at instilling classroom management skills. You can't pass your driving test by reading a book, and you can't hone classroom management skills without practice.

Possibly as a result, newer teachers say classroom management is their main teaching worry[4]. I also see lots of anxiety about future classes, stress caused by lack of time, and guilt when a lesson bombs. This is a shame, as a little time spent practicing the skills in this book can transform that your teaching practice.

Good classroom management benefits teachers with higher work satisfaction, less stress and lower blood pressure. Students benefit by being able to learn more efficiently[5].

6

Appearance

Good classroom management is invisible.

For new teachers, great classroom management is indistinguishable from magic. Everything in a lesson seems to flow. Students move naturally from one task to the next. There's no confusion or drama. When you teach at that level, observers will ask you why students 'just get on with their work' or why their class 'doesn't do that?'.

Classroom management also looks like learning.

As we saw in chapter 2, learning is the ultimate aim classroom management. So if learning is happening, there's a good chance you're doing classroom management right. You should feel proud when you see your students actively engaging in tasks, getting feedback and continuing to practice. You'll know that it's all your small decisions, habits and routines that allow learning to happen. Seeing learning happen is wonderful. It means you're making a difference.

7

Decisions

Classroom management is a series of decisions. Have you ever read a 'choose your own adventure' book? You know, the ones where you read then choose - option A, go to page 20; option B, page 32. As a kid I loved them, but I always cheated. I used my thumb as a bookmark, to flip back if my decision had terrible consequences.

Teaching is a 'choose your own adventure', and every decision moves the class forward. This time there's no cheating - you can't turn back after a poor decision. Another name for this is a 'decision tree'. You start from the same place, but there are countless paths through a lesson.

Although you've written a lesson plan, you still need to make lots of decisions in each moment of the class. There are many reasons. The material might be too difficult or too easy. Students might be tired. They might need to be more engaged. There might be interpersonal issues between students in a group. All of these might be unaccounted for in your plan, and need a quick decision.

It makes sense- you're interacting with real people, so of course you'll need to adapt. No lesson plan survives contact with students, to paraphrase an old military quotation[6]. This book is about the decisions that create those paths.

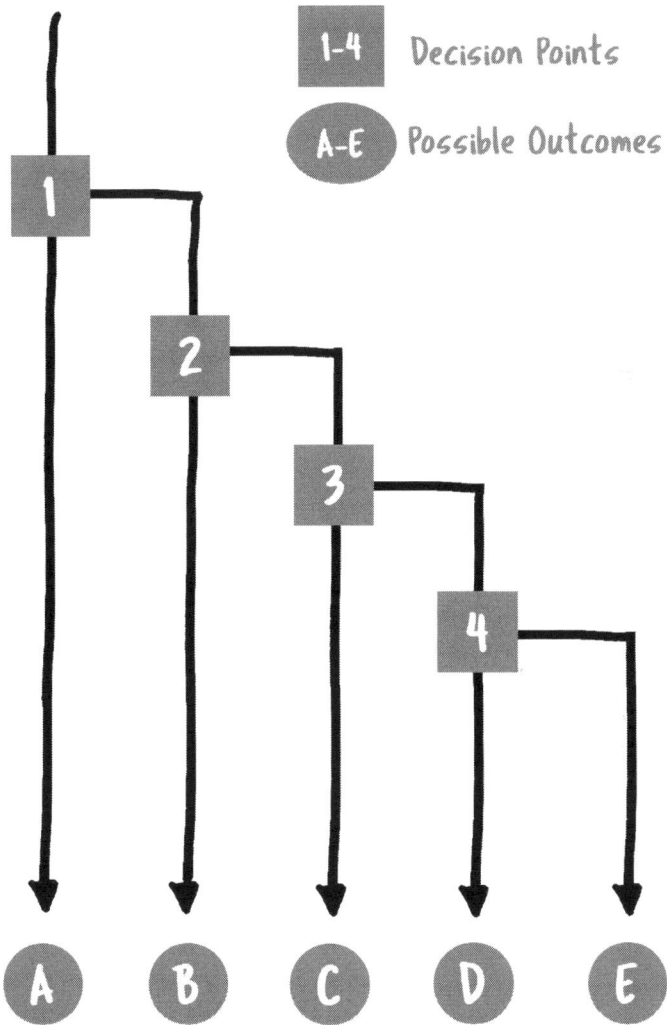

A decision tree – each decision changes the lesson

You build your teaching on thousands of decisions. Some you make consciously, some you inherit from your training, and some reflect your character. If you don't consciously make those decisions, then unconscious habits will rule your teaching. So many teachers have little idea why they do what they do - these teachers respond in the way they were trained (or instinctually).

In the heat of a lesson, you're under pressure to decide quickly. As you're learning, often you won't know the correct choice to make. Often there *isn't* a best choice, as you don't have enough information. But you have to decide and move forward, regardless.

The best teachers you'll ever meet (and the teachers who will become the best) are those who take time to analyse their decisions after a lesson. They consider how each action affected their students and their learning. This could look like three or four bullet points scribbled on a lesson plan, ready for the follow-up lesson.

So don't stop thinking and reflecting. Your decisions will depend on you, your students, your materials, and what you think will best affect their learning outcomes.

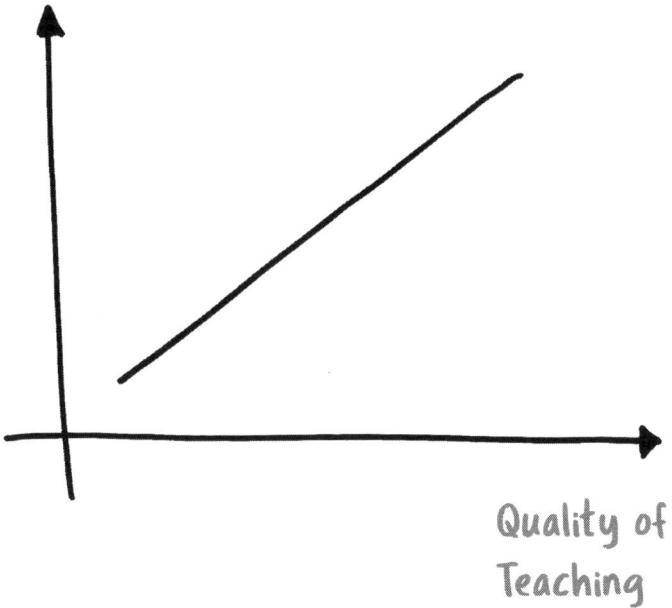

Quality of
Decisions

Quality of
Teaching

As your decision-making improves, so will your teaching

8

A Student's Perspective

Do you remember what it's like to be a student? Can you imagine what it's like as a student in your classes? Seeing from our students' point of view gives us clues about their motivations. Imagining with empathy can give us insight into how we should treat our students. Imagine if they were brutally honest:

"Dear teacher,

As a student in your class, I want to tell you a few things. Most of the time;

- I'm well behaved.
- I want to have fun.
- I may or may not be in the mood to learn.
- I enjoy talking and doing tasks with my classmates.
- I don't want to look stupid.
- I don't like using the course book, it sucks.
- I want you to notice when I do well, and get praised.
- I want my classmates to see how clever I am.
- Sometimes I like to poke fun at my friends, although I know it's wrong.

But if I don't understand or am bored,

- I'll play with my phone, classmates or ask to go to the bathroom.
- I'll start daydreaming.
- I'll feel stupid for not understanding.
- I might ask my friends what you mean, if I care enough. I probably won't though.
- You'll have to work hard to get my attention back.
- I'll think you're a bad/inconsiderate/uncaring teacher and resent you.
- I'll start to dislike your class (and maybe even learning!).

So that's me. Thanks for listening."

Remember to put yourself in your students' shoes occasionally.

II

Managing the Environment

9

A Positive Environment

Imagine you're a student walking into your classroom. How would you feel? Some classrooms make you smile, curious about what's happened and is going to happen. Others look like a bomb has hit them. I've taught in wonderful classrooms, awful classrooms, and everything in between. How would you rate yours?

No-one enjoys spending time in a messy, uncared for environment. From a learning perspective, the benefits of a great-looking classroom are considerable. We know that the aesthetics of an environment affects how we feel, and how students feel affects their attitude towards learning and classroom behaviour[7]. A classroom should feel safe, pleasant and be conducive to learning.

A well-organised physical environment also saves time. It's the biggest factor in the time a teacher takes to organise, direct and deal with unwanted behaviour[8]. Natural light and good air quality are the most important factor in learning, according to a study on environmental factors that affect learning in primary schools[9].

Where you can, personalise your classroom. From having the right sized chairs and desks for your students' age, to switching classroom layout for

25

different learning activities. Decoration can be a quick way to enhance a room (see next chapter).

There are some factors that we can't affect, of course. Depending on your teaching context, some situations we have to work around. It's hard to paint bare concrete walls with no paint or unbolt chairs from the floor. We can't reduce student numbers, or increase a budget of zero. For these situations, we do what we can.

10

Decoration

I used to be one of those teachers that spent hours decorating my classroom. I put up displays on every inch of every wall. There was students' work, learning displays, seasonal decorations – you name it, it was there somewhere.

I've relaxed my fervour. Now I know too much decoration can be distracting, I try to keep displays to a reasonable level. The question though, 'to decorate, or not to decorate' has been an ongoing debate for years. Some think decoration is a distraction, some think it's motivating. The answer – it depends!

For younger students or students with special needs, highly decorated walls and displays can be a distraction[10]. This effect lessens with older special needs students. Displays that have a significant effect on students are ones that include their own work. This makes them feel pride and a sense of community[11]. Unfortunately, other students' work doesn't interest them[12].

Displays meant to remind students of key learning principles aren't used much by students – even if they need that knowledge to compete a task![13] So choose your displays carefully. Here are some principles that have helped me decide what to use as decoration.

- If you put up students' work, make sure there's something from everyone.

Don't only put up 'best' work, unless you want to discourage weaker learners.

- Make it look good. Don't stick it directly to the walls, mount it on a cardboard background and add headings.
- Don't put up work that isn't student generated. If your students haven't helped create it, they'll ignore it.
- Add time to work on educational displays into your lesson plans for topical or seasonal ideas.

11

Layouts

No desk and chair arrangement is suitable for every activity. Each arrangement has a driving idea behind it, with inherent advantages and disadvantages. A useful way idea when considering layouts is the 'action zone'[14]. This space is where most of the teacher-student interaction takes place. Students sat in this zone often get more chance to interact with the teacher[15]. Be aware of this, and how to avoid it—by moving around the room, as appropriate, and interacting with all students the same amount, as far as possible[16].

Let's look at a few of the most common arrangements.

Traditional Rows

Driving Idea: that the teacher is the source of all knowledge and broadcasts this to the students.

Action zone: at the front / middle of the room.

Advantages:

- You can easily walk between the desks.
- You can see all students' faces and see if they're attentive.
- Students are less-easily distracted.
- Students can easily see the teacher and board.

Disadvantages:

- Students can't work in groups.
- Students can't easily have discussions.
- Students at the back may feel neglected.

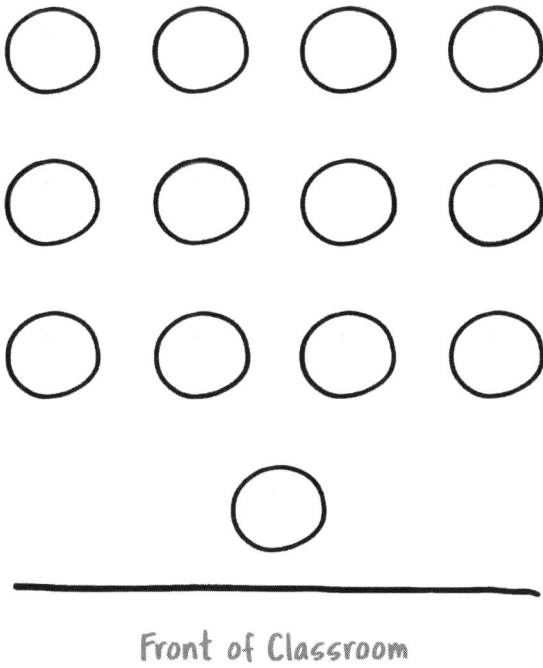

Front of Classroom

Classroom layout: traditional rows

Small Groups

Driving Idea: groupwork and collaborative tasks are central to learning.

Action zone: depends on preference – often at the front and in the most central 'row'.

Advantages:

- Students can easily work and talk in groups.
- You can easily talk to those groups.

Disadvantages:

- Gathering and keeping attention is trickier, as some students are facing away from you.
- Students facing away from you are harder to monitor.
- Students are more easily distracted by friends.

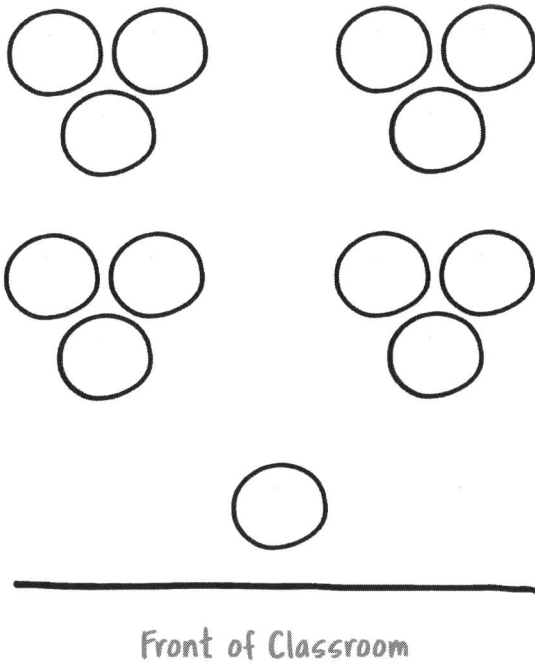

Front of Classroom

Classroom layout: small groups

Pairs

Driving Idea: pair work and discussion are central to learning

Action zone: at the front / middle of the room.

Advantages:

- You can easily move around and talk to pairs.
- You can see all students' faces and see if they're attentive.
- Students are less-easily distracted.
- Students can easily see the teacher and board.
- Students can form larger groups by one pair turning around.

Disadvantages:

- Partners can distract students.
- Movement is needed for a group discussion.

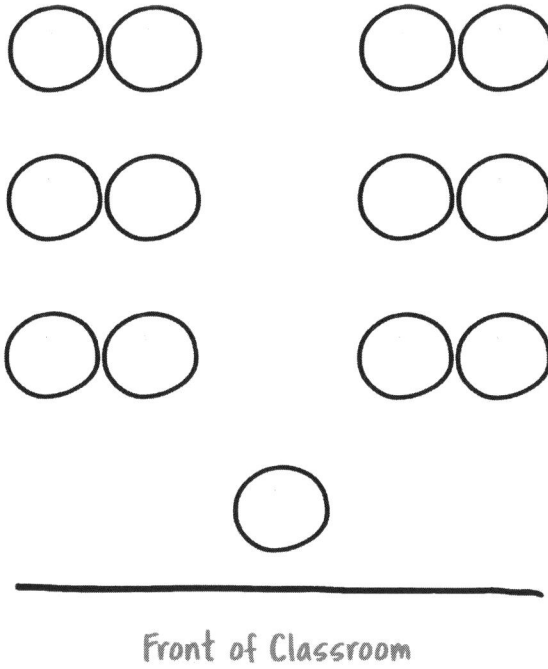

Front of Classroom

Classroom layout: pairs

U-Shaped (or Horseshoe Shaped)

Driving Idea: that collaboration and student to student discussion is central to learning.

Action zone: in the centre of the 'U' shape.

Advantages:

- All students can see the centre of the room, and the u-shape.
- It's easy for you to monitor students and see faces.
- Pair work is usually easy and doesn't involve moving desks.

Disadvantages:

- It's easy for students to distract others.
- Small group work is more difficult.

This may not be easy if the room is small.

12

Foot Traffic & Zones

Think about where students will be walking, and why. If you need students to collect items, do you need to set a one-way walking system in place to avoid a traffic jam? Is there a way to distribute those items across a wider area, perhaps on either side of the classroom?

Plan for times when large numbers of students are moving at the same time. Add it to the list of routines you can build into your lessons (see chapter 31).

If you're lucky enough to have space for more than chairs and desks, you can create 'zones' in your room. A great example is a space for reading. Think of the message a 'reading zone' sends, even if the books are a bit worn. An area at the front of the classroom could become a 'story zone', where students sit on a mat and listen to stories, or explanations. Or even a 'reward' zone, where students can choose a game to play at break time. Use your student interests to fire your imagination!

III

Managing Yourself

13

Body Language

The non-verbal signals you give, consciously or unconsciously, carry meaning which your students will pick up. Non-verbal signals give can set the tone of the class from the very beginning (imagine a teacher walking in looking angry and dropping books on their desk!). They can also have a profound effect on student behaviour, as students react and respond to you.

I strongly suggest that you film a few of your lessons. If you've not done it before, the first one you'll be acting unnaturally as you're super aware of the camera. Record a few more times, and you'll see how you really behave in front of the class, rather than how you think you act. Here are some common ways that you convey body language signals. Look for these on your lesson videos and decide if you want to make a change. If you do, work on one at a time, and record yourself to see your progress.

Posture

Self-confidence manifests itself in our posture. I'm sure you can easily visualise what a confident, in-control person looks like. Standing straight, shoulders back and chin up. Showing the opposite of this is an invitation to students to misbehave.

Eye Contact

Eye contact can be a sign of acknowledgement and respect. Balancing the amount of eye contact is also important; we interpret too much as confrontational (or just odd), while too little can be mistaken for a lack of confidence. So, make eye contact with every student during the class, but not so much that it's creepy. Make eye contact:

- When you speak directly to individuals.
- To acknowledge a student's actions.
- To notify a student who's starting to misbehave that you're aware of their actions

There could also be cultural considerations around the use of eye contact, depending on your teaching context.

Facial Expressions

Students are experts at reading teachers' expressions. They all seem to have an innate skill of knowing how far they can misbehave before they get into trouble. Thankfully, it's easy to use this to our advantage.

First, we need to make sure that all students can see our expressions to remove any ambiguity. So exaggerate them, although not so much you look like a clown! If student behaviour starts to deviate, show your displeasure–frown, shake your head, or however you normally would. Likewise, for positive feedback–nod your head and give a large smile.

Positivity

Positivity affects all aspects of your body language, and in ways it's hard to mimic. When you're tired and irritated, it shows. Likewise when you're happy and interested. Having a positive expectation for a lesson and a group of students has a very different vibe than if you walk in expecting to have a bad lesson. So stay positive - look for the good in each lesson, in each student and have a personal goal for every class. It'll keep you challenged, engaged and curious, which translates into positivity.

Non-Verbal Signals

Non-verbal communication is a powerful tool to convey signals to your class. Some are by facial expressions or positivity (see above) but others can have different functions. Some signals can start or stop an action or routine. For example, clapping your hands once to gather attention, or gesturing with two hands which two students should work as a pair.

Be aware of non-verbal signals you use naturally, and if you find them useful, commit to using them regularly. Over time, they remove the need to speak as much, which can keep the lesson flowing. Non-verbal signals can be especially useful during error correction, and we'll talk more about that in chapter 37.

Presence

I'm sure you remember which of your teachers had a 'presence' from your school days. I think every school probably had a 'domineering' or scary teacher, and a warm and friendly 'mother' figure—both of whom inspired good student behaviour.

You don't have to become either of those figures to gain respect or deliver an excellent class. Presence comes from confidence, experience, personality and correct classroom management – so you can start by applying the ideas in this book, and your presence will grow.

14

Emotions

The primary driver of your body language is your emotional state. If you're enthusiastic, happy and full of energy you'll bring your best to the lesson. That's a very different you than when you're stressed, unhappy and tired. Following suggestions from the last chapter will work to an extent, but faking genuine emotion is hard.

Controlling your emotions is the key to leading your students' emotions. You lead your students by example–if you're excited, calm, curious, bored or annoyed, then there's a good chance they will be too. Strong emotions are infectious, and students will sense them and respond accordingly. Here are some tips to control and maintain your emotions.

Before Class

I've lost count of the times that I've *really* not wanted to walk into my classroom to start a lesson. Rather than bring any negativity in with me, I've paused, breathed deep and put on my game face. 'Game face' isn't a new concept, but changing your frown a to a smile, throwing back your shoulders and walking confidently into the room means the battle is half-won. This, or anything else, can be a pre-class ritual to calm your mind and prepare yourself. Find what works for you!

During Class

Never lose your temper. If you do, you lose the connection with the class. It often escalates the situation. For some students, they see it as a 'win' to make the teacher lose their self-control. Remember to breathe into your belly, relax your face and de-escalate.

After Class

Congratulate yourself on what went well, acknowledge what didn't and what you can do to improve your performance next time. Balance being positive with yourself and giving a realistic assessment.

15

Speech

How you speak *and* what you say are crucial to having a great lesson.

There are several variables with speech - how long you speak for, the complexity level of the language you use, how fast you speak, how concise and clear you are, and the intention behind it. That's lots to consider, but we can break it down to make it easier.

You may notice that some teachers have a 'teacher voice' - slower, deeper, and more authoritative than when they speak one-to-one. That's a 'teacher voice'. Let's look at what you can do to improve your teacher voice.

Speed of Speech

If you talk too fast, you'll appear nervous or overly excited and students might mentally 'check out' and lose motivation to listen. If you're not sure, speak slightly slower than you think you should, and remember to breathe into, and 'speak out of' your stomach.

Length of Speech

Keep it as concise as possible, as long as it doesn't affect clarity. Keep it short when you're giving instructions, explaining or correcting. You can take longer when you're telling a story or anecdote-you don't want to rob an anecdote of its flavour. Adapt to the situation.

Project Your Voice

Speak to the students at the back of the room to make sure your voice carries. There's no faster way to lose a class than if they can't hear you. Breathe deep, from your belly, rather than into your chest to help with this.

Personalise

Although this is more related to the content of your speech, rather than the way you speak, it's still worth mentioning. Make sure that you've personalised something for the students. It could be a reference to something you know they like, or are interested in. A popular movie, celebrity, local attraction or great restaurant, etc.

Intention

Have a reason to speak and don't be afraid of silence. If you're just filling time, you'll appear rambling and unfocused.

16

Grading Your Speech

Every day well-intentioned teachers walk into class and sabotage their students' learning. They do it unconsciously. They do it by not monitoring the language they use when talking to students. Language that is:

- Too difficult (too much unknown vocabulary, too colloquial, etc)
- Too fast
- Too many discourse markers (um, er, y'know, OK, etc.)
- Too much 'echoing' (which means repeating the students' responses back to them, like an echo)

I've observed a couple of teachers who had at least seven uses for the word 'OK' (they were using it to mean: start / that's fine / yes / no / stop / do you understand? / good).

Don't make your wording too complex. Use words that you're sure your students will understand. Likewise, for older classes, make sure you raise the complexity, as they don't want to feel that they're being patronised.

Improving your spoken language is simple to fix, although not easy. Just record yourself with an audio recorder in a lesson. Most smartphones can record a whole lesson quite easily, you don't need an audio recorder. Record your lesson and listen to it later.

Now listen to it from the point of view of one of your students. Do you speak clearly? Do your instructions make sense? Are there any irritating habits? If you're like me, you may be surprised at the sound of your voice, your speech habits, the way you talk to your students – it can be eye (or ear!) opening. A classroom language a tune-up can work wonders on your class control.

17

Talk Time

Teacher talking time (TTT) has a poor reputation. It's easy to see why—as teachers talk more, the amount that students talk usually decreases. An extreme version of this is a 'lecture' style class, where the teacher talks 100% of the time, and students 0%. No matter how dedicated your students are, not being able to interact or communicate is boring. This hurts students' motivation and willingness to communicate in class.

So first work on grading your language (see previous chapter). Make sure you're not over-explaining, getting sidetracked, or rambling. What's left should be crisp, concise and functional language to run your classroom.

However, there are reasons to increase your teacher talking time. After all, a purely functional classroom can be boring. So consider increasing your talking time for two reasons:

1. Building rapport
2. Storytelling

Building rapport is the foundation for everything good in your classroom, as we'll see in chapters 23 and 24... and how can you expect to build rapport without communication?

Similarly, storytelling is huge, and can have a transformational effect on your classroom. Not the, 'here's a life lesson I learned from the pub, off-the-cuff' style story, but pre-planned, language graded, context relevant and intriguing story. Used wisely, it's a great way to personalise the topic, and add colour to otherwise boring lessons.

So consider extending your TTT at strategic times. Everyone wants to feel respected and everyone wants to know how a good story ends.

Teacher
Talk Time

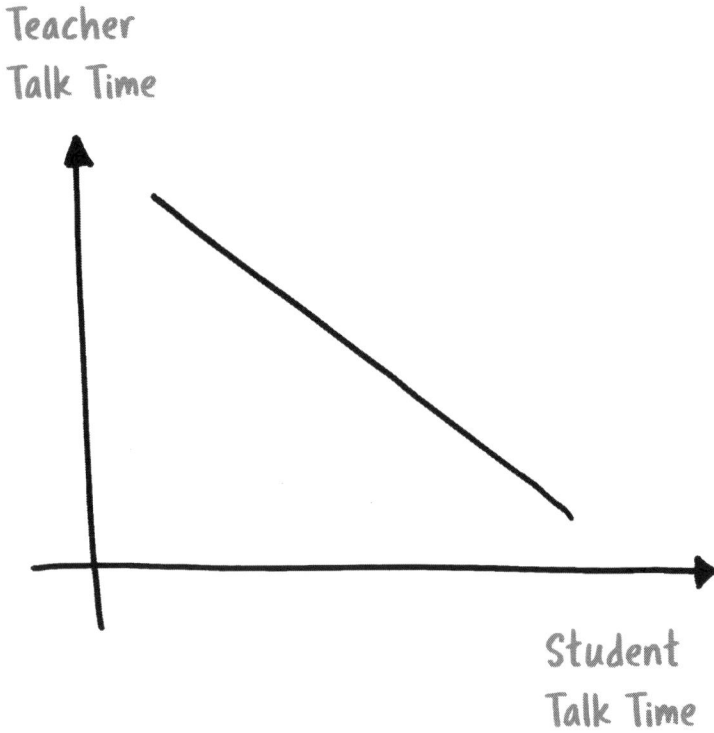

Student
Talk Time

As your talking time goes up, there's less time for students to speak

18

Silence vs Noise

Often newer teachers are taught that discussion and collaboration are the only times when learning occurs. As a result, silence becomes something to avoid. However, silence can be a useful tool and I'd like to show you four ways to use it effectively.

'Critical Thinking' Silence

A study showed that pausing for longer after you ask your class a question can increase the quantity and quality of the responses you get[17]. A further study showed that waiting for longer increased both the quantity and quality of student responses[18] (A longer waiting time before answering allows students to engage their critical thinking skills. So, pause for longer (3-10 seconds) after you ask a question. It might seem awkward at first, until students adapt, but don't be afraid of the silence.)

'Cooling Down' Silence

After a fast-paced activity, it's nice to create a quieter, calmer atmosphere before moving on to a different activity. It allows students time to transition from one topic to the next. An example could be one minute of silence to review what they know about the upcoming activity.

'Creativity' Silence

We ask students to produce creative result the second we ask them, and then complain that they have no imagination when they fail. Give the students some quiet, contemplative time to think! After you give them a task, allow silent thinking time. Make sure they know how much time that they have, so they don't feel the need to rush.

'Concentration' Silence

When you want your students to concentrate on a critical point, a tricky problem, or even to emphasise a point, use silence. It gives time to focus and think, and perhaps take notes.

19

Awareness

I'm sure you remember a teacher who could magically detect whispering, daydreaming, or off-topic behaviour, no matter how tiny. These teachers were masters of 'withitness'[19], an awareness of what's going on around you in the classroom.

Sometimes called a teacher's sixth sense, or 'having eyes in the back of your head'. All I know is that the teachers that had it seemed like ninjas. It's an extremely practical skill - teachers who have more awareness are able to spot minor misbehaviour earky are able to stop it escalating. Which means, of course, that they're less likely to have disruptions in their class[20].

So how do you develop withitness?

Be confident enough of your ability to deliver a lesson that you're not focusing on minor things. Rather than trying to remember what to do next or finding a misplaced book, you can raise your head and be aware of your surroundings. A lot of confidence comes from lesson planning in enough depth that you develop that confidence.

Next is deliberate practice. It's easy to let a lesson pass and forget to focus on being more aware. Think of developing withitness as a personal aim for each lesson.

Lastly, it's common sense. Minor misbehaviour often happens at predictable times during the lesson, from predictable students. Students will try to sneak a quick chat, or get distracted when you turn to write on the board, or when you pause for too long for any reason. Notice what happens in the small gaps in your lesson. Good luck!

20

Overlapping

Research shows that multi-tasking doesn't exist. Instead the brain switches rapidly between inputs to give the impression of focusing on more than one thing simultaneously[21].

However, when we're teaching, interruptions happen frequently, forcing us to 'multi-task', or switch rapidly between issues. In a teaching context, this has been given the name 'overlapping'[22].

When interruptions occur, our priority is to continue the lesson for the majority of students while attending to the interruption quickly and effectively. This requires assessing the priority of the interruption, and dealing with it appropriately.

Some you can deal with quickly, some will need you to gather everyone's attention. Some you can deal with non-verbally, some will need varying levels of escalation (see section 7, 'Managing Behaviour' for more ideas). Your focus should be how you can resolve the issue with minimal disturbance to the lesson.

As with awareness (see previous chapter), this is a skill to practice consciously.

IV

Managing Relationships

21

Connection

Relationships are the engine that drive learning. Learning in school typically involves a student, a topic, a teacher, the student's peers, parents, the environment & the topic material. The more connected a student feels to each of these, the better the environment is for learning.

If a student feels strongly about a topic, they'll look forward to it, enjoy reading and listening about it, and want to engage in lessons on that topic. They might even engage in it for fun, outside of the classroom.

However, if the topic materials are boring, it will gradually suck the life out of the topic for that student. Conversely, if the materials are bright, engaging and pitched at the right age range, then the student's connection and passion is reinforced. The same is true for the way a teacher presents the subject -in a boring manner, or with endless testing, the students will lose the joy of learning.

If a student's friends all think that the topic is silly and pour scorn on the student, they'll probably disengage. If the student's friends approve and think the subject is worthy of praise, the connection between student and subject is further reinforced. A similar pattern is true for the student's parents' attitude towards the subject. Peer pressure is powerful.

These variables make up the environment your students learn in. Is it a positive, welcoming one, or the opposite? Consider these variables, and which ones that you're able to affect as a teacher. The more you're able to influence, the better your classroom experience will be.

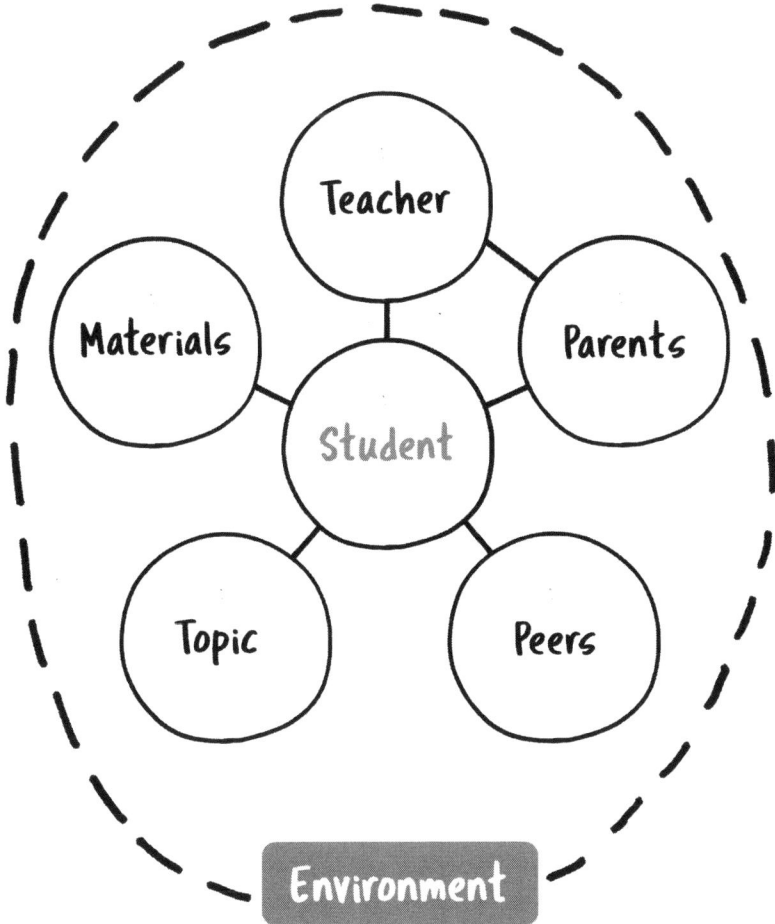

The key relationships involved in student learning

22

Student-Teacher Rapport

Many students study and perform better for teachers they like and respect[23]. This is especially true when you build rapport and personalise lessons for students.

Building an environment where students feel psychologically safe is the key to them relaxing and not worrying about making mistakes. Students need to take risks to learn and they won't in an environment they perceive as unsafe, or with a teacher they don't trust. The first step to accomplishing this is building rapport.

Building rapport is one of the most important things you'll do in the classroom. Establishing rapport with students motivates, inspires, and leads to creativity, learning and enjoyment in the classroom.

Imagine two teachers, with the same practical and theoretical skills working in the same school. The only difference is that Teacher A doesn't care about building rapport, whereas Teacher B does. Let's see what happens.

Teacher A

Teacher A starts his first term full of enthusiasm. During his first classes, he launches straight into the coursebook, eager for his students learn everything by the end of term.

Although initially enthusiastic, he notices that students become gradually disinterested. Asking students what they think draws blank stares most of the time. It seems he's got a tough class!

Slowly non-interest turns into mild misbehaviour. Although his classroom and behaviour management is good, students take every opportunity to test him. Classes turn into a battle of wills.

Halfway into the term and it's all-out war. All but the most obedient students ignore him and misbehave. While he's trying to encourage students in one corner, misbehaviour erupts in another. Well-prepared activities consistently go off the rails. The time for an observation comes, and Teacher A is flagged as having quite serious issues with class control. The end of term approaches, and on parents' evening several parents have issues with their students' performance.

Teacher A is seriously thinking about quitting – he no longer enjoys his work and has to force himself into the classroom.

Teacher B

Teacher B also starts her first term enthusiastically. Instead of rushing straight in with the coursebook, she spends the first few lessons to better understand her students. She plays 'getting to know you' games, she remembers their names, she talks to them (and they talk to each other). They discuss what they enjoy doing, how they like learning, what they expect from their teacher, and what a teacher should expect from her students.

During subsequent lessons, she arrives to class early and talks to students about non-lesson related stuff. She doesn't just sit at the front of the class, but next to students (the good ones to praise them, the weaker ones to help, and the shyer ones to draw them out).

Teacher B makes some procedural errors, and isn't the best teacher, but students like her and are forgiving of her mistakes. She engages mostly in activities that encourage collaboration between students, rather than competition. More importantly, she's able to relate the lesson topics to the interests she knows they have, rather than just using the dry coursebook. Students learn better and faster as a result.

Sure, there are some minor infractions, but the behaviour management system holds up and there are no serious problems. Teacher B praises student behaviour to one or two parents when she sees them around the school. An observation by an academic manager shows that she's doing well. When parents' open day comes around, parents are all happy and there are no issues.

Teacher B decides that she loves teaching and looks forward to the next term.

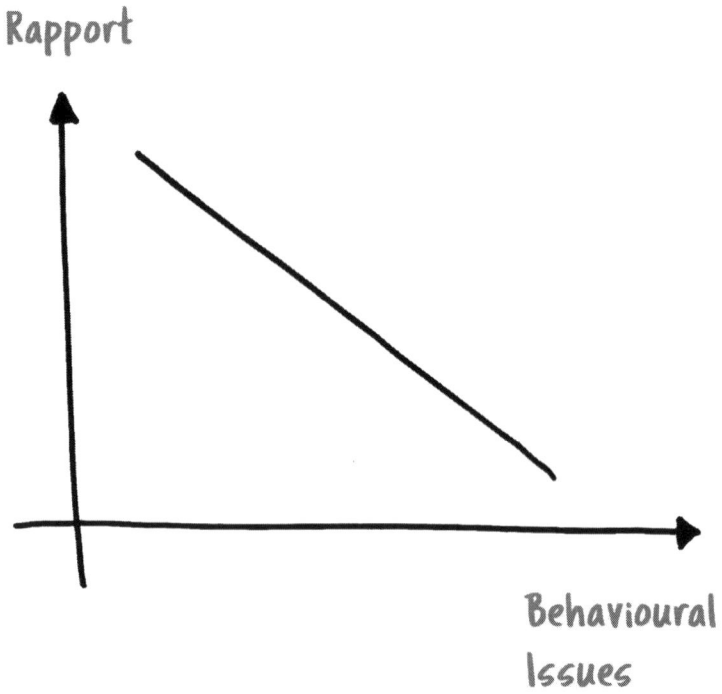

As rapport grows, you'll notice behaviour improves

23

Building Rapport

There are many ways to build rapport, but there's one secret behind all of them: you have to care. If students can see that you genuinely care about them, they'll respond. If you try to follow any step-by-step 'how to build rapport' system, it can come across as mechanical and fake, if you don't care.

Some people use humour in the classroom. Some talk about their hobbies. Some arrive to class early to talk about non-school topics. Others do none of that, yet can still show they care through their actions and words.

One thing they all have in common is that they respect their students. Respect your students as individuals and understand that they aren't an amorphous mass 'to be taught'. If you give them respect, they'll most likely respect you back.

Respect is the first step. Knowledge and time spent together are the second and third. The more you know about your students, and the more time you spend in the classroom with them, the more you're likely to care about them. Once you genuinely care, trust yourself—you'll know how to respond appropriately. Although just in case, here are some simple tips.

- Be genuine—students know when you're not.

- Be humorous–but not too often, you're not a clown!
- Be kind–you never know what students are experiencing outside of class.
- Be thoughtful–notice and give attention even to the quiet students.
- Be helpful–and encourage helpfulness in your classroom.
- Be honest–give honest feedback, but kindly, so it'll be well received.
- Be generous–with your time. Arrive to class early to talk amiably.
- Be collaborative–choose collaborative activities over competitive ones.

Building rapport gives them motivation, which gets them to learn, which gets them results. Focus on rapport and motivation, and you can get out of the way and let them get on with it by themselves.

Remember to care, and you'll enjoy teaching so much more!

24

Student - Student

Another aspect of an ideal learning environment is how students interact with each other. Students will follow your lead in how you treat other students, and peer pressure influences how they respond to you, the topic and the tasks. Here are three principles that you can use to improve student-student relations.

Be Inclusive

Include everyone in your lessons, even the shyer students, or students that take longer to answer. Remember that students have their own lives and struggles that you know nothing about, and be patient. Set tasks that promote collaboration and cooperation, not competition (see chapter 30 for more on this). This gives the message that in your classroom, you value everyone equally. See chapter 28 for more.

Set Minimum Standards

You may want to outline rules of behaviour or ask students to set their own. Be sure to ask how they should treat each other and add that to the rules. See chapter 41 for more on setting classroom rules.

Reward Ideal Behaviour

Reward the behaviour that you want to see in your class - volunteering, trying your best, taking risks with learning, and being kind. Don't reward negative behaviour, selfish, mocking, or being overly competitive.

25

Parent - Teacher

Building rapport with parents can be extremely useful. Although it doesn't seem like a crucial component of teaching life, it can make a big difference to your students' learning outcomes. Plus, it'll make your life easier.

Having parents on your 'team' to work with and support their child's learning is a powerful tool. It provides a consistent support network, sets expectations, and gives the message that the key figures in a child's life prioritise learning.

Your school policies dictate how many times you have to interact with parents. Events like parent meetings, reports, school events, and so on. All these events have their own procedures, and you'll have time to prepare for them. This means you should give a good impression, but being under time constraints means it's difficult to build rapport.

So take the time to interact with parents whenever you can. Spare a few moments if you see them in the foyer. Say hi outside the school gates and give a few comments on their child's progress. Praise good behaviour or a recent effort. You can always excuse yourself politely if you get entangled. By the time the next formal event occurs, parents will hold you in high regard and take your suggestions more seriously.

26

Student - Materials

If students find their learning material boring, they'll look for something else to do. Where possible, use material that you think your students will find more interesting than the coursebook.

It's impossible to make every lesson fascinating for every student. But there are ways to improve the odds of more students engaging with the lesson through interesting (for them) material.

Start small, by personalising examples that you use in class. Use stories, analogies, news, computer games of celebrity gossip that will interest your students. Make up the shortfall with imagination and creativity.

More ambitious is replacing actual coursebook examples and materials. If you regularly teach the same subjects, then creating new materials can be an investment as you can reuse them again at a later date.

V

Managing Engagement

27

Engagement

After building rapport and relationships, students are ready to listen. If you respond by delivering the most boring classes known to humankind, you'll lose the goodwill and rapport you've built.

Managing engagement means ensuring that once you've got the students' attention, you can focus it on something for a sustained period. The more you can do this, the more positively it will affect your students' learning outcomes. The next three chapters will look at some ways to do this.

Learner
Engagement

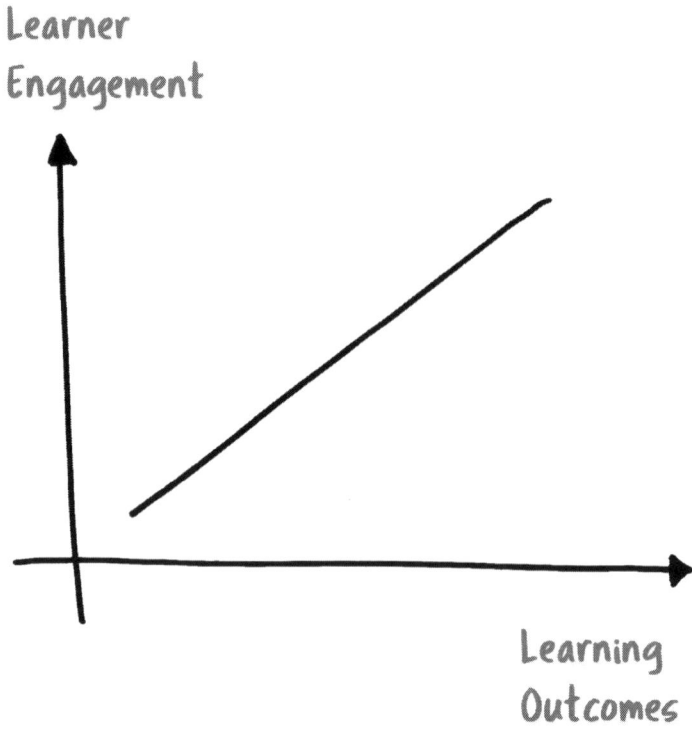

Learning
Outcomes

Better engagement means better learning. You can't learn what you don't think about

28

Inclusion

Be sure to include all your students as equally as possible. It's easy to pay more attention to the noisy ones, the clever ones, the enthusiastic ones and the naughty ones. The problem is that then you neglect the quiet, shy, and introverted students.

The first step is to be aware of this. The second is to include them *sensitively*. Suddenly asking a shy student to stand and give a speech in front of the class isn't positive inclusion. Instead, think of how you can give them attention and support with less pressure. Can you exchange comments as you circulate, or make sure they're taking an active role in group-work?

Lastly, try not to develop favourite students (or at least don't show who they are!) and never discuss students with another teacher where they might hear.

29

Variety

Variety is an important part of engagement, but you need to balance variety and routine. Not enough variety leads to boredom, too much can lead to confusion. To balance variety and routine, create routines for classroom management activities (see chapter 31), and create variety in your learning materials and activities.

Create variety in activities and materials by personalising the topic and your materials (see chapter 34 and 35 for ideas). It sounds like a chore, but creating variety is the fun part of planning and teacher!

If you're struggling for ideas for personalisation, talk to colleagues who've taught the same subject or same students as you. Ask them for their 'never fail' activities, the ones that work every time with minimal preparation.

Variety in materials is tricky without spending lots of time and effort adapting the set course materials. One way is to use 'student generated materials', where you ask students to bring in or create relevant materials that you can use (and then reuse for later lessons).

You can also create personalisation and variety through changing course examples to ones that resonate with students, draw comparisons and analogies that are familiar and interesting to them, and use examples or stories that they find funny. Be careful to still follow the curriculum, hit the required standards.

Another way to add variety is through adding more interaction. Most students enjoy talking to their friends over reading a dry coursebook. As a resource to engage your students, their peers are unrivalled, so make use of them.

Take the time to see if you can adapt individual activities to those involving pairs or small groups. The reward is a room full of engaged, focused students working together to complete a task.

Of course, not all students work best with others. So, make sure that when you do have individual work, you personalise these tasks to your students' interests as much as you can.

30

Competition vs Collaboration

Some teachers say competition is evil and only use cooperative activities. Others regularly use competitive, see great results, and wonder what the fuss is about. So which is better?

Wrong question–they're both just tools to be used appropriately. Cooperation is usually good; competition can be good or bad, depending how it's used.

Here's a quick summary:

	Advantages	Disadvantages
Competition	• Can add interest to a boring topic. • Activities are easy to prepare and run. • In teams, can promote group skills. • In some cases, can add healthy motivation.	• Moves focus from learning process to outcome. • Can lessen students' intrinsic motivation. • Can increase anxiety. • Can decrease peer relationships • Can decrease. creativity and problem solving.
Cooperation	• Students learn important social skills. • Weaker students can be supported. • Less pressure on students.	• Can take teacher longer to prepare. • Can be harder to assess cooperative efforts. • Weaker students can 'hide' in a group. • Stronger students may get frustrated that they're not recognised individually. • Tasks must have a 'gap' to encourage cooperation.

Advantages and disadvantages of collaboration and competition

Healthy and Unhealthy Cooperation

Healthy Competition–is fun, it's short, it's high-energy and the stakes aren't high (i.e. there aren't any long-term consequences of losing).

The Golden Rule of Competition / Cooperation

I've always followed a simple rule for using cooperation and competition, and it's stood the test of time:

'Use cooperation to learn, and competition to review.'

This hits the advantages and avoids the disadvantages of both, most of the time.

VI

Managing Activities

31

Setting Routines

Classroom routines keep you and the students sane. It's counterintuitive, but they don't make the class boring, they free up time and mental energy to allow for the fun stuff. Routines can be your best friend because they:

- Saves time and energy (both yours and the students').
- Helps shyer students' confidence.
- Works wonders for behaviour management.

Imagine two teachers; Teacher A doesn't have any routines, but good Teacher B does.

Teacher A

Teacher A does things differently every time. Not a lot, but enough that he has to explain and the students need to use some of their limited reservoir of attention to listen. All this takes time. The students often get it wrong too, especially the younger learners and the lower-level learners. This leads to more time error-correction. The students misbehave as their attention wanders.

Teacher B

Teacher B has routines for all those activities. When she starts a new class, she takes time to explain her routines. This is how we store our bags under our chairs, that is how we take attendance, this is how we divide into pairs, and so on.

Before long, Teacher B is flying through lessons as students know what to do and how to do it. Behaviour is good as expectations are clear at transition points.

Teacher A still struggles with getting his students to do what he wants them to do. As a result of this lingering uncertainty, behaviour is still an issue, and classes are that much more tiring. Which teacher would you rather be?

Here are some questions to prompt reflection on your current routines, and situations where you might want to clarify them.

Start of Class Routines

- How do students enter the classroom?
- How do they prepare for the start of the lesson?
- Where do they store their coats, bags, books and stationary?
- How do you take attendance?
- How do you collect homework?

During Class Routines

- How do you setup tasks or activities?
- How do you give instructions?
- How do you pair or group students?
- How do you check understanding?
- How do you correct different types of errors?
- How do you finish a task or activity?
- How do you move from one activity to the next?
- How do you respond to bathroom visit requests?
- How do students get your attention to ask a question?
- What's your policy on mobile phones usage?
- What do students do if they complete a task early?

End of Class Routines

- How do students react to the bell at the end of the lesson?
- How do they pack their things?
- What's the procedure for leaving the classroom?

You'll find out what best works for you as you try new ideas. Change routines slowly—too many changes at once can cause chaos! Give students time to adapt before changing another. I'd also suggest observing your colleagues or asking them for their most effective routines. Pick and choose what works best for you!

32

Giving Instructions

Activities are the heart of your lesson, so it's worth spending time to give them the best chance of success. Activities are where the learning happens, and also where you'll be spending most of the lesson time. They're also the most complex part of any lesson, and so take time to master.

Giving effective instructions is crucial to running a successful activity. If you don't get your instructions right, your young learner classroom will probably degenerate into chaos.

To make giving instructions easy every time, I like to use four simple steps:

1. Show
2. Tell
3. Ask
4. Give

(Which makes the acronym STAG, to make remembering easier).

Show

If possible, model the activity. Show them what it looks like.

Where sensible, let students help you do this. If it's a dialogue, ask a capable student to help you role-play an example. If it's a worksheet, show an example on the board.

When you show a good (or great) example, you set the standards. This gives a good chance of better quality student work, as most become aware they can't scribble and hope.

Tell

Grade your language so that the students will understand you.

Are there any words that they won't understand? Substitute them. Also, drop the 'um, er, yeah, like, OK' fillers, to sound more confident. Simplify and shorten your instructions. How can you say what you need to in the minimum number of words? If this is tricky at first, spend 5 minutes to plan what you want to say before the lesson.

Stage your instructions, and turn them into a list. Hold up your fingers for emphasis as you count through them, i.e. "1–complete the question on page 10. 2–you have five minutes to finish. 3-when you finish, compare your answer with your partner's". Turning instructions into bite-size chunks means students are more likely to remember them.

Ask

You've set the stage and filled their brains with instructions. Did they listen? Did they understand? You'd better find out before you tell them to begin.

I've found the question "What do I want you to do?" works well. If you used a numbered list for your instructions, ask different students for different numbers (Adam, what's the first thing I want you to do? Tina, what's the second?). Make sure that weaker students understand (but don't always pick on them to answer, the class will catch on).

Don't ask 'do you understand?' Students will either say nothing, or 'yes', just for a quiet life. Either way, you won't truly know if they understand.

Give

Now, finally, you can give students any materials they need to complete the task. You can let them re-arrange their chairs, or move positions if required.

33

Interaction Patterns

Interaction patterns describe how many students are working together. Usually we talk about:

- Individual work (working on their own)
- Pair work (two students working together)
- Small group work (3-5 students)
- Large group work (5+ students)
- Whole class (everyone in the class)

A good rule of thumb is to use a variety of these patterns throughout the lesson. Too much of one interaction pattern and a lesson can be boring. Too many changes, and it can distract from the lesson itself.

I like to put my interaction patterns in a sequence, to either support students, or encourage them to be creative. This is shown in the diagram below. The two arrows represent two ways of sequencing your interaction patterns. 'A' starts with the whole class, and then reduces the size of the groups as the task or lesson progresses. 'B' is the reverse.

Don't feel that you have to use every stage of the pyramid–it would be overkill. I rarely use every stage. It's more of a directional suggestion.

Sequence A

This provides excellent support for challenging activities. By starting with the whole class, students get to practice in a 'safe', less pressured context.

Moving from whole class to large to small groups, students assume gradually more responsibility for the completion of the task.

Sequence B

Starting with individual or small group work is a good way to prepare for a larger group or whole class activity, e.g. a discussion or a debate.

Students can think ideas through by themselves and form their own opinion. They can then exchange ideas in a small group, sharpening their ideas or abilities, before engaging in a larger group or the whole class activity. A great sequence for any complex task-based activity.

Interpersonal Relationships

The social dynamics of a class make or break it, all other things being equal. In some contexts, it's standard practice to pair a stronger student with a weaker student, so the stronger student can help the weaker one. This sounds good on the surface, but after a few lessons of this, how does the stronger student feel? Happy and willing to help? Or frustrated, annoyed and totally unwilling to take part? It could be either, depending on their personality. This is where you as a teacher need to monitor how students are interacting with each other and try to spot trouble before it blooms.

Some students don't work well together, others do. Cliques form and change.

Stronger students like to work with others of their level, others don't. Some love the responsibility of being called on to help peers. Others hate it. Naughty students' excess energy can be channelled for a force for good (teacher's helper anyone?), while shyer students need extra encouragement from you.

So be aware of your students and use your awareness to help the smooth running of the classroom.

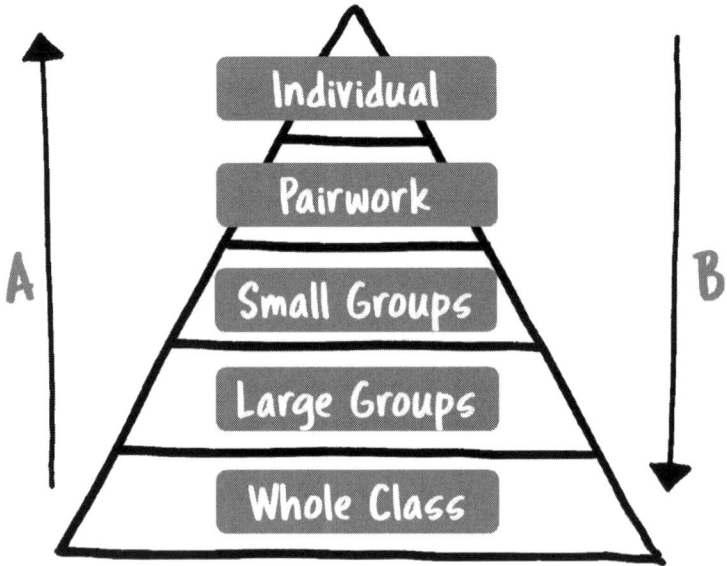

Two example sequences of interaction patterns

34

Differentiation

Differentiation is a method of teaching one concept and meeting the different learning needs of a group of students[24].

Differentiation is a scale. At one end is teaching 1-to-1, where everything is 100% personalised for one student. At the other end is treating every student the same, regardless of their ability or needs. Your job as teacher is to move as close to the 1-to-1 end as possible whilst juggling all of your other duties (and your sanity).

We differentiate because students are people, not statistics. If the material is too easy learners are bored, too difficult and they're quickly demotivated. Students are different ages, genders, and come from different geographic and cultural backgrounds. All have their own personalities, ideas and interests. So why would teaching them all the same way make any sense?

You can start differentiating with a new class, but the better you know your students, the more effective it is. As far as possible, know their character, their strengths and weaknesses, their background, their interests and their interpersonal relationships in the classroom.

There are six ways that I differentiate. They're straightforward, relatively simple to implement and I've used them successfully for years. I differentiate by time, by task, by topic, by material, by grouping, and by role.

By Time

Have an extension task ready for stronger learners that finish a task early.

By Task

Adapt tasks slightly, based on student ability. A good way to set more challenging tasks is to move up Blooms' Taxonomy[25] for the same set task (e.g. instead of showing that they understand it, ask students to apply it. Or instead of asking them to apply it, ask them to analyse it, and so on).

By Topic

Adapt tasks by topic. This means to personalise the content based on interest. If half your students are interested in tennis, and half in swimming, can you give phrase the activity or task using a topic related example?

By Material

Materials can provide differing levels of support. By editing your materials before the lesson, you can cater for different student abilities (and interests!)

By Grouping

If you group learners of similar ability together, it makes it easier to differentiate and provide relevant support. It helps you monitor, set differentiated tasks, topics and hand out differentiated materials (assuming students are grouped appropriately).

By Role

If you pair weaker and stronger learners together, you can stronger learners a different role in the group. Perhaps as group leader, or error-checker where they have extra responsibility besides the task.

35

Scaffolding

'Scaffolding' is support that we give learners by breaking down a task into manageable chunks[26]. By providing support, then gradually handing over more and more of the task to them, students will move from dependency to independence.

> *"What a child can do today with assistance, she will be able to do by herself tomorrow."*
> *– Lev Vygotsky[27]*

The idea of scaffolding came from Lev Vygotsky, a psychologist in the early 20th century. He described a zone of what students already know, a zone of what they don't yet know, and a zone of learning. He called this the 'Zone of Proximal Development'[28]. He proposed that in this learning zone, students learn more effectively with help from someone (or something) more knowledgeable, compared to learning on their own.

Today, scaffolding involves breaking down a task, skill or activity into parts, then give support to learners to master each part, and then the master the whole. Scaffolding is also viewed as a way keeping high standards for all learners, rather than 'dumbing down' the class for weaker learners, an accusation that's been levelled at differentiation (when it's done badly).

How to Scaffold

Think about the task you'll ask your students to do. Write a numbered list of the stages they'll have to go through to complete it. Now consider the difficulties they'll have at each stage, and what support they might need. This could include things like:

- Further explanation
- Explanation in a different format (by video, infographic)
- Individual practice
- Practice with others
- Worked examples
- Analogies

With these, the idea is to link target knowledge with students' current knowledge.

Does Scaffolding Have any Disadvantages?

Only if it's misused. One way that this can happen is if the lesson and tasks are 'over supported', i.e. if too much help is given. If that happens, then you'll most likely see learners get bored and start to rely on the support, rather than think for themselves. How do you know if it's too much? If your learners can't answer a question without referring to support material at the end of the class, it's too much.

Top Tips for Scaffolding

- Know your students' level
- Monitor closely (you can keep an eye on the level of challenge)
- Don't offer too much help, or students will come to rely on you.

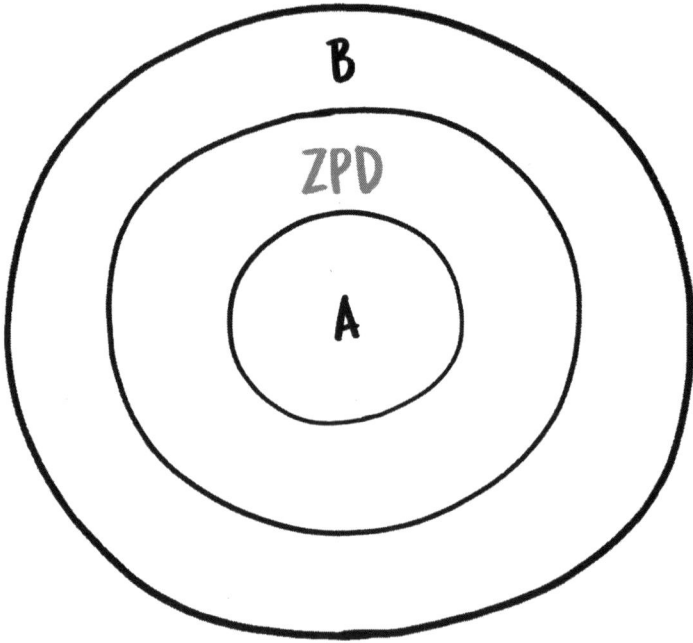

A: Within student's ability
B: Beyond student's capability
ZPD: Zone of Proximal Development
(within student's capability with
assistance)

The 'Zone of Proximal Development'

36

Timing & Pace

Timing & Pace

Timing is how long it takes to complete each activity and stage. Pace is how fast it feels for students as they progress through activities. Is it too fast and they're struggling to keep up? Is it too slow and they're bored? Or is it just right, and the level of challenge is maintained?

Timing

Timing can be tricky. Even experienced teachers have trouble getting the timing right in every class. My golden rule for timing is:

> *'Everything will take longer than you plan it to, even when you take this rule into account.'*

A common mistake is to overfill your class with content and activities. I'm sure you've had this happen to you! You get overexcited when you plan the class, and only cover about half of the content by the end of the lesson.

There's nothing as disappointing in finishing a class just as the students are just starting to grasp the concept and using it as you want them to. So leave 5 minutes or so as a buffer in each lesson. You'll find this is often used for transitions and other classroom management aspects. Even if not, it's usually simple to extend a final activity for a few minutes.

Pace

Keeping the pace of the lesson so it keeps everyone interested is tough. You need to walk the line between quick enough to keep your advanced students interested, and slow enough so all your students understand. This is why differentiation is important (see chapter 34).

It's one way to help with engagement and motivation also - if you see students getting bored (when they've just been attentive) then speed up. If they're looking confused, slow down, and check their understanding.

Lastly, remember that you can make easy activities more difficult if you increase the pace, and difficult activities easier by slowing down.

37

Error Correction

It's a good sign if your students make mistakes. It shows that they're engaging with the material and testing ideas, which will lead to learning. It's your job, however, to correct errors and ensure that learners remember and understand the correct aspects. The best error correction has three elements.

1. **Timeliness**
2. **Personalisation**
3. **Reformulation**

Timeliness

Correct as close to the error occurring as possible. The dilemma happens when students are in the middle of a dialogue. Do you interrupt to correct them and risk derailing the conversation? Or correct later when it's less effective? Or write down general class errors and do a review at the end that covers 'most' of them?

Personalisation

The correction is tailored to the student's individual error, rather than giving generic whole class feedback (students never think general advice applies to them). How do you find the time to do this for every student, though?

Reformulation

The student has a chance to try again until they get it correct. Which is fine for confident students, but the pressure of having others waiting for you to correct yourself can destroy confidence - especially when a student is trying to scan what they've just said for an unknown error.

Effectiveness of Correction

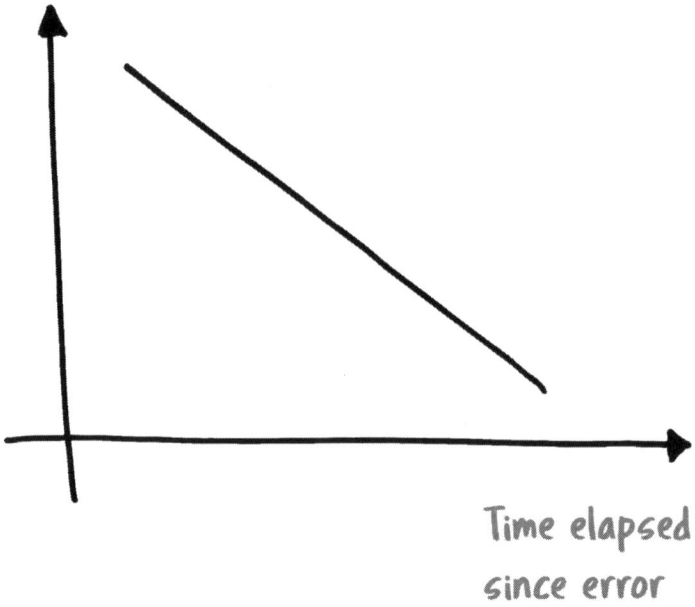

Time elapsed since error

Error correction is more effective the faster it is given

38

Error Correction Hierarchy

When you notice a student error, your brain goes through a process to decide if, when, who and how it should be corrected. Usually it's subconscious and you respond in an instant. It's useful to pull this out and examine it, so we can improve how we correct errors and become aware of our own routines.

Should You Correct?

The first step we ask is whether we should correct an error. Depending on your subject (e.g. language teaching), if you corrected every student error, you wouldn't have time for anything else. You should correct an error if:

- It's an 'on-target' error—an error critical to understanding the target topic.
- It's a 'high-frequency' error (i.e. an error that students make frequently)
- It's something that students should know already, that affects this topic.

If it's an 'off-target' error, i.e. one that's not about the target topic for this lesson, then you can decide if correction is necessary. You can also choose to correct the student during a quiet moment.

When Should You Correct?

The second is when to correct. Errors can be corrected straight away (immediate error correction), or later at a more appropriate time (delayed error correction).

In general, you should correct on-target errors as soon as possible, and it may be worth stopping an activity to make sure that all students are aware of the correction (otherwise students may continue practicing incorrectly!)

Correct off-target errors as soon as you can, especially if many students are making the same error. It's probably not worth interrupting a task that's running well to do so. If it's just one or two students making the error, then you may wish to notify them at a quiet time sometime later in the class. For off target errors that are low frequency, you may wish to notify students individually, later, or ignore for the moment. As with all of these, use your common sense. Don't overload the students, but also don't let their errors fossilize.

Who Should Correct?

Ideally, the student that made the error should correct themselves. If you ask a question, they may realise what they did wrong and make the adjustment.

If not, getting another student to correct can be a great way to correct an error (assuming learners are familiar with each other and not afraid of losing face). Either through partner activities (students have to give their partner a token every time they make an error), to small group activities (students try to make a presentation with zero errors), there are choices to get students to cooperate. The last choice is an explicit correction from you, the teacher.

How Should You Correct?

If you're raising awareness for the student to self-correct, then you can either say something to show that the student has made an error, or you can use a non-verbal signal. Some common ones are raising an eyebrow or looking surprised. You can even agree a system with your students, so that when you give a non-verbal signal (i.e. tap a pen) they know they've made a mistake.

For correcting written errors, your subject may have a list of error codes (i.e. shorthand notifications for showing where and which mistake was made). Remember to ask colleagues for their best error correction techniques as well!

Should you correct?	• Is it on-target? • Is it high frequency?
When to correct?	• Immediate correction • Delayed correction
Who corrects?	• Self-correction • Peers • Teacher
How to correct?	• Non-verbally • Verbally

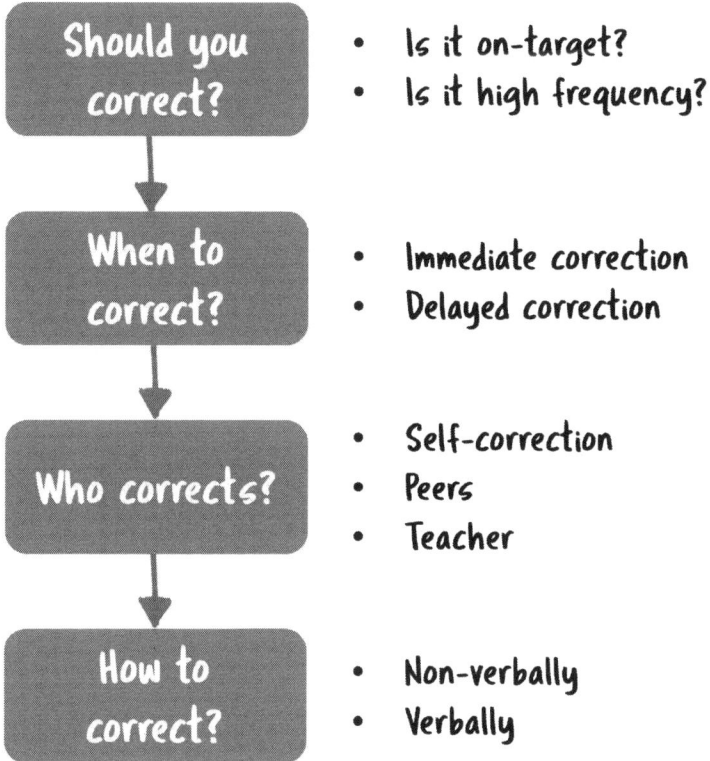

An error correction hierarchy

39

Transitions

Transitions are the change from one activity to another. There are three general types of transition; starting a lesson, moving from one activity to the next, and finishing a lesson.

Transitions are a perfect time for behaviour to go off track. They're a natural pause in the lesson, when students are moving from one thing to the next, and unless you capture students' attention and focus it, it will wander to other areas.

Watching an otherwise fantastic lesson go off the rails because transitions weren't handled well is heartbreaking. Transitions fail for three reasons:

You Didn't Have Their Attention

If you transition out of an activity when students are still engrossed, it'll be a struggle to get everyone on the same page again. Letting them know how much time is left can mentally prepare them for the coming change. Also give them a regular signal that you want their attention (clapping hands, using the same phrase).

Too slow, or Too Fast

If a transition takes too long, students will get bored and attention will wander. If transitions are too fast, you can 'lose' students, or confuse them and they'll start the next activity not sure what they're doing (or why).

Too Many Instructions, or Too Few

This is related to 'giving instructions' (see chapter 33) – make your instructions concise and clear. Too much direction will have them fidgeting, too little instruction may leave them confused. Remain observant and check that all students have confidently started on the new activity. Finally, remember to make use of student routines, especially start and end of class routines (see chapter 32).

VII

Managing Behaviour

40

What is Behaviour Management?

Behaviour management is avoiding or managing unwanted behaviour with classroom routines. It's one aspect of classroom management, but arguably one of the most important.

Yet, with a rock-solid system, you can deal with anything that happens in your classroom. Students know what to expect and see you treat them consistently and fairly. You gain more respect, and they gain a teacher they can trust.

There are two broad types of misbehaviour: minor misbehaviour and serious misbehaviour. Minor misbehaviour is casual and opportunistic. It happens when students become distracted, or bored. Its primary cause is students is an absence of focus, times when there's a lull in the lesson's flow. Time a teacher spends handing out worksheets or writing on the board. Minor misbehaviour is low-level disruption and can usually be dispelled by the teacher re-focusing the class.

Serious misbehaviour is often more deliberate. A student makes a choice—either conscious or not—to act inappropriately. It can escalate from untreated casual misbehaviour or be a spontaneous or premeditated incident.

Misbehaviour is better prevented than managed. The first step to preventing it is to set expectations and classroom rules, which we'll look at next.

41

Expectations & Rules

A famous study showed that when teachers have higher expectations of students, those students perform better and have improved learning outcomes[29]. This became known as the 'Pygmalion effect' in psychology, and has been shown to be true across many fields of performance. The reason behind it is straightforward - if a teacher believes that the student can achieve the task, they unconsciously treat the students differently. Perhaps they wait longer for an answer, give more positive praise, more detailed feedback, smile more, or any of many other ways that help students to internalise these expectations.

Unfortunately, the reverse is also true. If a teacher has low expectations of a student, they will internalise that worldview instead. As a teacher, students can see when you don't have faith in them, and it crushes their confidence. Off-hand remarks, not caring to correct errors, a raised eyebrow here, an eye roll there... students see it, and take these unconscious messages to heart.

So be a teacher that cares and set high expectations for your students. Show disappointment if you can tell they've not put effort into a task. Conversely, praise them for trying hard, even if the result isn't what they hoped for.

One way of setting expectations with a new class is by agreeing classroom rules as a group. It can be a great exercise to get to know your students. Ask your students what rules they would like. Put them in small pairs or groups to discuss. At first they'll laugh about rules like 'no homework days' or 'come to school dressed as a superhero' rule. Guide them by asking them how they'd like to be treated in class—by you and by each other. Ask them how they think they should treat you as the teacher.

The wording varies, but common sentiments remain similar for most classes. They want to be treated with respect, they want to be listened to and they want to feel safe and happy. Many teachers choose to have a classroom 'contract' written up and signed by all, then displayed on the wall. It can be a powerful visual reminder for students throughout their time in your class.

42

Preventing Misbehaviour

If you've followed the steps so far, you've improved the classroom environment, your habits, and the way you manage student relations, engagement and activities. By doing this, you've already prevented most of casual misbehaviour- congratulations! However, there are still some things that you can do to make sure you prevent as much unwanted behaviour as possible.

Before Class

You win half the behaviour management battle when you plan your lesson. During planning, ask yourself:

- How are you going to build or maintain rapport with your students?
- How are you going to make sure they're engaged?
- How are you going to manage the activities you've planned?

The eagle-eyed among you will have spotted that these are earlier sections in the book. Use each of these sections, and their chapters, as a checklist when you're planning. The key is to make sure there are no gaps in your lesson plan, no cracks for the weeds to grow through.

During Class

There are four areas to be aware of when working to prevent misbehaviour in class[30]. These are

1. Withitness
2. Overlapping
3. Signal continuity and momentum
4. Variety and challenge.

We've already looked at withitness in chapter 19, 'Awareness'. The message is that the more aware a teacher is, the harder it is for minor misbehaviour to get a foothold. Be as aware of your classroom as possible.

We looked at overlapping in chapter 20. To remind you, this is the ability to switch between doing multiple things quickly, or 'multi-tasking' to keep the lesson on track.

Signal continuity and momentum are the ability to maintain the flow of the lesson. Always make sure that your students have something to focus on. Ask them to discuss a question with a partner while you prepare for the next activity. Have them start completing a worksheet before you start writing at length on the board. Any transition between activities should be smooth, with no time for distractions. Don't give any 'dead' time outside of activities for unwanted behaviour to occur. Also maintain an appropriate pace for the lesson – not so fast that students get confused, and not so slow that students get bored.

The last is variety and challenge, which we looked at in chapter 30.

After Class

Ask yourself how well the lesson went. Assess yourself against all you've read so far and pick one area to work on in your next lesson. This doesn't need to take long. Just go with your gut as to what didn't work as you hoped, and jot down some ways you could do things differently next time.

43

Minor Misbehaviour

Minor misbehaviour includes students talking, daydreaming, or anything behaviour that's not 'on task' and that's not too disruptive. When you notice it, you have a choice of whether to correct it (sometimes it's best not to). If students exchange a few brief words while getting books out of their bags, they'll probably focus again when you start the next activity. Making a response in that situation might be more disruptive than letting it go. Too much discipline, especially jumping on every minor infraction, would be exhausting and quickly erode any rapport you have with students.

Another instance that you might choose to ignore behaviour is if you can tell a student is misbehaving just for the attention. If that happens, ignore them, and give them attention and positive reinforcement when they tire of acting the clown and begin to work again. You can often understand the intention of students by picking up on the clues they give. If get to interpret the behaviour and decide if it needs a response. Afterwards, you can also reflect and see if you were right.

When you do decide to intervene, it's usually best to start with non-verbal correction and move to verbal correction only if you have to. Here's a list of the most common ways to intervene:

Move closer to the misbehaving student.

Why it works: most students will know that you're there because you're checking on their behaviour, and they'll stop misbehaving.

Give students 'the look'.

Why it works: the students is fully aware you've caught them red-handed, and they'll self-correct.

Use other facial expressions.

Why it works: this is the same principle as (2). You can also use it for positive reinforcement or praise.

Gesture the students.

Why it works: using hand signals to signal the student(s) to stop their misbehaviour / model the correct behaviour is unambiguous direct communication.

Removing distracting items.

Why it works: by removing a distracting item you remove the source of distraction and remind students they should be working.

Give positive reinforcement.

Why it works: giving praise is giving attention, and misbehaving students crave attention. Giving this attention to well-behaving students shows misbehaving students that their attention-seeking tactics don't work. Further reinforce by giving them praise when they've returned to good behaviour. One student can be praised or all good students.

Use the student's name.

Saying a students' name is a way to tell the student that they're aware of their actions. Good to use if a student is so distracted they wouldn't notice any of the previous techniques.

44

Serious Misbehaviour

Serious misbehaviour requires more than the simple interventions we've seen so far. The single biggest difference in how you respond to serious misbehaviour is that you'll impose a consequence on the student.

For minor misbehaviour, the interventions can be short, almost unnoticeable, and allow the class to continue. Serious misbehaviour requires your full focus, so the class will probably pause while you address it.

Before this, let's revisit what we mean by serious misbehaviour. I've found a useful definition to be *'any behaviour which significantly impacts on the ability of learning to take place'*. For me, this can also include minor misbehaviour that is persistent, as it disrupts learning.

When you decide to treat behaviour as more serious, you'll be intervening and delivering a consequence to the student(s). As such, it's more disruptive to the lesson, and so should be used sparingly.

Consequences should follow 'the three Rs' rule[31]. These are:

- **Related** – the consequence should be related to the misbehaviour (e.g if they deliberately throw litter, they could be asked to clean the classroom).

- **Respectful** – it should be respectful of the student, not humiliating or harmful.
- **Reasonable** – it should be corrective, so they know what to do in future. It shouldn't be punishment 'to get revenge'.

Let's look and see what an example hierarchy of consequences would look like in the next chapter.

45

Hierarchy of Consequences

Some schools have explicit systems to deal with serious misbehaviour that they expect all teachers to use. Others leave it to the teacher to decide how to respond. Some have standard responses only once behaviour has reached a consistently unacceptable level, such as detention, suspension or expulsion.

Check to see if one exists at your school. They may have rules in place for excessive behaviour (e.g. for asking the student to leave the class, seeing the principal, or what constitutes contacting the student's parents).

A standardised behaviour management system can feel restrictive as the procedures may not fit with your 'style' of teaching. One major advantage, though, is consistency for students. They know what will happen if they misbehave, regardless of which teacher they're with.

A hierarchy of consequences will differ depending on the students' age, the teacher preferences (and any school policies in place).

For primary school students, a simple hierarchy might be:

1. A warning

2. A time-out (choose an appropriate time, usually 5-10 minutes)
3. Taking them aside and giving them a consequence (see 'Minor Misbehaviour' chapter).
4. Contact parents (either verbally or in writing)
5. Send students to the head teacher's office

For older students, you might substitute the time-out for staying behind after class for two minutes.

For new teachers, I'd suggest asking your academic manager for examples currently running in the school, and experienced colleagues for their favourite techniques. That way you're automatically 'fitting in' with the culture of your school, and students will already be familiar with the routines (saving you time and energy!)

Lastly, remember to always agree your system with your academic manager.

46

Consistent Misbehaviour

The techniques we've covered in minor and serious misbehaviour will work for most students. There will still be times when you have a student that consistently misbehaves. With students like these, you need a stricter method. An effective method will use a written agreement, a tracker, consequences and rewards, and positive reinforcement.

You should negotiate a written agreement with the student (or with parent and student together). Remember to emphasise why you're doing this—it's not punitive, you care about your student and their learning! The agreement should outline the expected standard of behaviour, a reward for meeting it and the consequences of not. The reward and consequences should be something that are significant for the student, otherwise this can fall flat.

Next, create a visible way to see student progress (or lack of). This could be marks, house points, stickers or something else. The student receives the rewards or consequences as agreed. The visibility acts as a consistent reminder to all.

Finally, when the student's behaviour starts to change, give them positive reinforcement- praise them in front of others, give encouragement and attention. Make the emotional benefits of being on the right path clear.

VIII

Managing Learning

47

Teaching vs Learning

Managing learning is regularly checking that students are understanding and able to use the material you've been teaching them. Even if every other aspect of your classroom management is perfect, if you're not regularly checking their progress, how can you be sure all your combined efforts aren't being wasted?

Often we congratulate ourselves after a lesson that seemed to go really well, only to find students remember nothing the next lesson. Good rapport, engagement and well-run activities don't guarantee that learning happens. The last piece of the puzzle is to check that learning is actually happening in our lessons.

The first way to ask 'concept-checking questions' when your students encounter new concepts (or when they revisit old ones after a while). Instead of asking 'do you understand', you'd ask specific questions. After you've introduced a new animal (e.g. a sloth), you'd ask where it lived, what it looked like, how fast it moves, what it eats, and so on. Make it a practice to sprinkle concept-check questions around the class when you're not sure students will understand fully.

The second way to check if learning happens is to test. Assessment can be summative (a more formal 'exam' type test) or formative (checking as learning continues). Formative assessment can take the form of monitoring what students are doing, asking questions, and engaging in dialogue with students so you know what they're thinking. Remember that students only remember what they think about[32]. So check in with them regularly, ask them questions, monitor, and use the 'thinking routines' in the next chapter to see and hear what's going on in their heads.

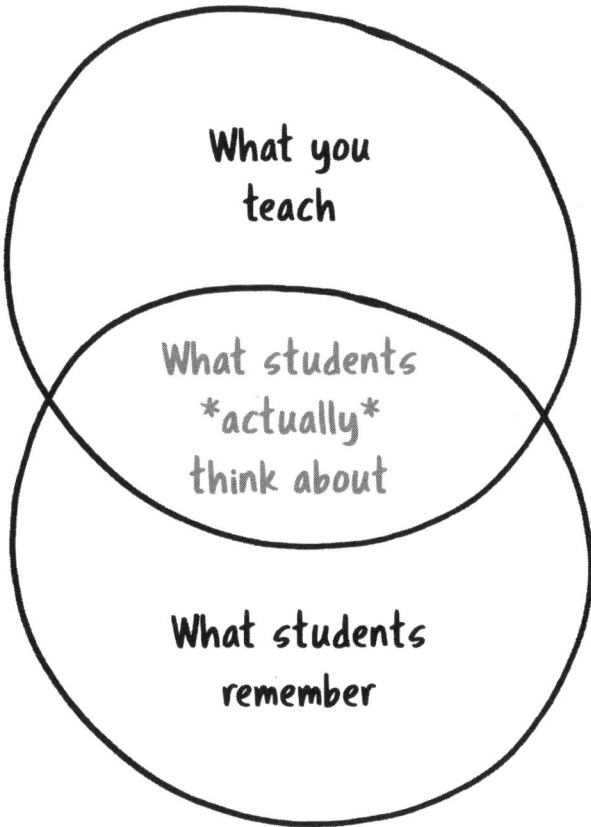

Students remember what they think about

48

Thinking Routines

A thinking routine is a brief series of steps that guide your thought process. They're simple and easy to use. When we talk about routines in the classroom, we usually mean the basic physical and social routines that we've seen in chapter 32. Thinking routines take the idea one step further and apply the idea of routines to learning. They are ways you encourage your learners to process information for learning and interact intellectually.

Encouraging students to use them regularly will lead to them growing in confidence, improving critical thinking, and being more open to discussions. Finally, for us teachers, thinking routines often make the thought process visible, so we can see learning happen. It's like when we 'show our working' in a maths problem - we can see and hear the steps students are taking as they go through our lessons.

In some form or another, thinking routines have been used in teaching for a long time. However, a formalised approach to collecting and classifying these seems to have come from Project Zero, a Harvard Graduate School of Education project[33].

There are at least 65 defined thinking routines, although several of them are for specific subjects. Here I'll share some of the most common, thinking routines that are adaptable for multiple uses.

1. 'Think-Pair-Share'

In this thinking routine, learners:

- **Think:** about their response to input (a question, a problem or a situation)
- **Pair:** discuss their thoughts in pairs.
- **Share:** their thoughts with others.

2. See-Think-Wonder

- What do you see?
- What do you think is happening?
- What does it make you wonder?

See: Show the students an image, object or video clip – anything that's inherently interesting!

Let them watch or observe, and think silently to form their own opinions. At this point they shouldn't be interpreting what they see, just noting things that they could 'touch' in the image / video.

Think: Ask your students what they think is happening. What do they think? Why? What makes you think that? What else is happening?

Wonder: What does this make you wonder? What questions does it make you ask? Be careful that students don't ask if their thinking from before is 'right', but they expand their wondering to broader issues.

After each stage, it's a good idea to allow students to talk to each other to compare their ideas. Pairwork or small groups are ideal.

3. Think-Puzzle-Explore

This is great for activating prior knowledge, wondering and planning.

- What do you think you know?
- What puzzles you about this topic?
- How can you explore the topic?

Think: ask your students what they think they know about a topic. Give students time to think. You can ask students to share, and then new ideas might emerge from the sharing.

Puzzle: ask students what questions they have, or what puzzles them, about this topic. You can help facilitate by asking further questions, such as what would be interesting to learn about the topic, which aspect is curious, and so on.

Explore: ask students how they could go about finding a solution or an answer. Who would they ask? Where would they find more information? What would the first step to solving the problem be?

This can be done and shared in small groups or pairs, or presented to other groups at the end.

Think → Pair → Share

See → Think → Wonder

Think → Puzzle → Explore

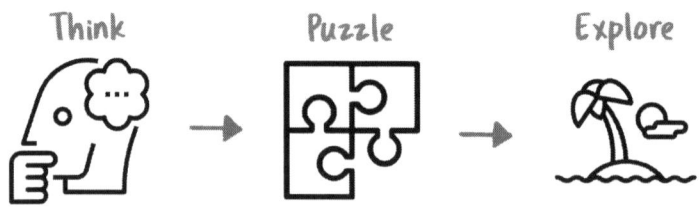

Example 'Thinking Routines' 1

4. Compass Points

This is great for discovering personal opinions, making decisions and planning. It starts with the points of the compass:

- E = Excitements: What do you find exciting about this topic?
- W= Worries: What worries you about it?
- N=Needs: What do you need to find out?
- S=Stance, Steps or Suggestions. What's your stance? What are the next
  steps? Or what suggestions do you have?

I usually do this routine in pairs, to encourage discussion at each step. You
can do it individually, but it'll only practice writing.

To set up the activity, you'll need large pieces of paper on each of the four
walls, one for each of the compass points. Students will stick their writing
to it later. Give the students a prompt - could be an event, an image or video
clip, a statement or question. Anything you like!

E = Excitements: Ask the students what they find exciting about the topic.
What's positive? Give them time to discuss in pairs, then jot down notes. If
they're not excited, ask why other people might be. Then ask them to post
their ideas on the 'E' paper.

W= Worries: ask the students what worries they have about this topic and repeat the process for 'E'.

N=Needs: ask the students what they need to find out to know more and repeat the process.

S=Stance: same for the students' stance, or ask them for their suggestions and / or next steps.

If your classroom management [link] is on point, you can divide the students into four sections, and have each section start with a different compass point. Then, when they post their thoughts on the paper from the second time onwards, they'll be able to read others' opinions and discuss in their pair.

5. Chalk Talk

Good for finding out prior knowledge and ideas, and questioning what students know. Great for writing practice and giving everyone a chance to share their ideas!

- What ideas do you have about this topic?
- What do you think about other people's ideas?
- What questions come up as you think about these?

For this routine, make sure you choose a good starting word, phrase or question.

Present: Share it with the learners (on the board). Ask them to think about the ideas or responses they have to the prompt and write these down.

Circulate: Students pass their papers to the person on the left. Give them time to read, and then you can either ask them to write their response to it (and continue to circulate) or have conversation aloud with the original writer (they'll need to take turns).

Facilitate: as the teacher, be aware that you'll need to help weaker or quieter students by suggesting or hinting at ideas, giving useful comments and helping when students get stuck.

If the learners are weaker, it's a possibility that they can work in groups of a similar level. Just be aware of weaker students 'hiding' and letting others do all the work.

6. Connect-Extend-Challenge

This is a great routine for making connections between ideas, finding new ideas and generating questions.

- How is the topic connected to what you know already?
- What new ideas did you get that extended your thinking?
- What challenges or questions have come up from the new ideas that have been presented?

Choose a story, reading excerpt, video or similar that will interest learners. Tell students they'll probably be learning something new and tell them you're going to ask them how it connects to their current knowledge.

Connect: Show / read the chosen subject, and ask students to jot down what they thought, and how it connects to their current knowledge.

Extend: ask them how their thinking has extended or changed. Jot down, discuss.

Challenge: ask students challenges or questions have come up from the new ideas that have been presented?

You can ask students to discuss in pairs or small groups after each stage.

Benefits of Thinking Routines

- They're easy to use and require no extra training
- They make the thinking process visible which can give solid example to weaker learners. This support can help support their own thoughts.
- They can create a culture of critical thinking in your classes.
- They are adaptable – you can use most for any topic or skill that you're focusing on.

Compass Points

 E: Excitements
W: Worries
N: Needs
S: Suggestions

Chalk Talk

Present  Circulate  Facilitate

Connect  Extend  Challenge

Example 'Thinking Routines' 2

49

Cognitive Load

Cognitive load theory explains how we process and remember information, and how too much (or too complex) information is harmful to learning. In this article we'll look at cognitive load in our lessons, and 5 principles to reduce cognitive load for our students.

As teachers, cognitive load theory is a key principle that should inform teaching decisions we make, as it can critically affect our students' learning outcomes. Sometimes abbreviated to CLT, cognitive load theory came from research into problem solving by John Sweller[34]

Sweller built on previous research that showed that working memory has a limited capacity and described the relationship between working and long-term memory. This diagram shows the rough process of processing and remembering information:

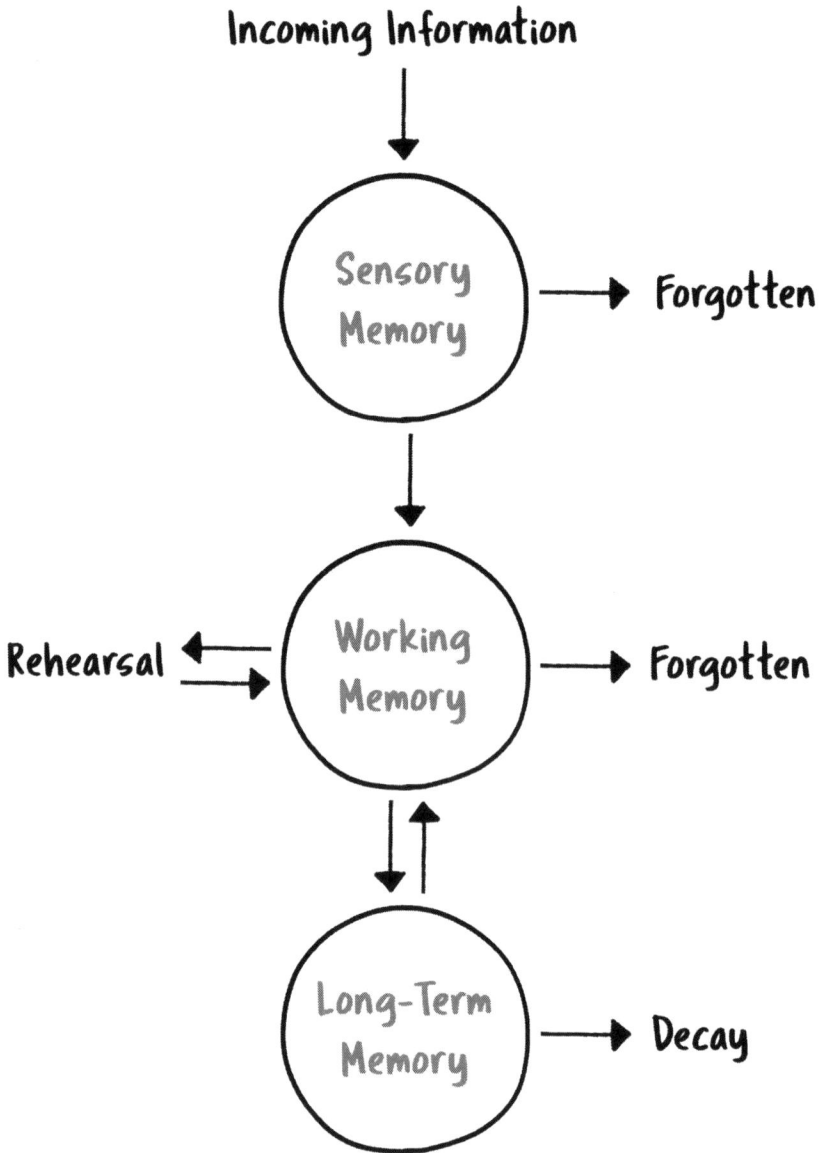

A simplified information processing model of the brain

As you receive information, the senses pass some of it onto your working memory, while some is ignored (you can't take in every detail in your field of vision!). Your working memory might rehearse the information for clarity (or not), then it's processed (or encoded) into your long-term memory. The same is true in reverse, when you recall information that you want to use. Your working memory acts like a gatekeeper, as it works hard to filter all the information it receives and decides which to keep.

Unfortunately, working memory isn't that large (some people have said it's like the RAM on a computer, whereas the long-term memory is like a hard drive). So working memory can suddenly become a bottleneck when it hits its processing limit. When our students are learning in our lessons, there are several ways that we can overload their working memory. Let's look at the different ways this can happen. Cognitive load types fall into three broad types.

1. Intrinsic Cognitive Load

Intrinsic cognitive load is how complicated the topic or task is. Calculus is innately more difficult than simple addition, and most would agree that the present simple is easier to grasp than the third conditional. The intrinsic load is higher in these tasks because the complexity is higher.

2. Extraneous Cognitive Load

Think of extraneous cognitive load as extra information that distracts from the key information you want to get across. Too much information, too confusing, or unnecessary information. We see this in the classroom as overly complex or badly designed materials, or a noisy environment (or even overly complex teacher instructions).

3. Germane Cognitive Load

Germane cognitive load looks at how easy it is for students to link their current knowledge to the additional information. It's part of the processing that takes place as the brain encodes the information into the long-term memory.

5 Principles to Reduce Cognitive Load

Richard E. Meyer developed these in a 2002 paper[35] . Remember them when you're planning your lessons and in the classroom!

1. The Coherence Principle

Reduce the amount of information to only what's necessary. Keep things simple and clear, and focus on clarity over style. This typically applies to two key areas in a class:

- Materials (where possible!). Don't write unnecessary instructions. Make sure images are clear and unambiguous.

- Teacher Talk (e.g. giving instructions). Grade your language to their level. Don't overload students with too much information when you speak. Leave room to think when you ask them a question.

2. The Signalling Principle

Highlight important information somehow. Draw attention to it. Applies to both spoken and written information. When you speak, alter your pacing. Pause dramatically. Whatever you do, don't speak in a monotone.

3. The Redundancy Principle

A classic example for this is reading the information from a screen. While it might be necessary to present information in different formats for your students, do it because they might need it, not because of lazy teaching. Don't keep repeating instructions when students already 'get it'. Same for language points that they've already mastered.

4. Spatial Contiguity

Show things related to each other, close together (or at least show that they're linked). For materials, if you're labelling a diagram, you try not to add the label three pages after the image. Make sure you link items and their meanings close together.

5. Temporal Contiguity

The same as (4), but with time instead of space. So link related concepts close together, without leaving large time gaps in between. In conversation, you wouldn't suddenly jump to a topic from 10 minutes ago without warning and expect students to understand!

When presenting language to learners, it's better to present linked items (I.e. an image of an item and the name of that item) together, as soon as possible. For both temporal and spatial aspects, it helps to present language in context. This is fantastic for helping with germane cognitive load, as it automatically links the information to a relatable situation.

Finally, don't make things too simple. I've seen teachers go to extremes and make things so simple that it affects clarity. Materials that are too simple become hard to understand because they're ambiguous. Overly simplified spoken language can become grammatically incorrect or be a bad language model. The key is moderation.

Germane Load
(linking new
info with
current info)

Intrinsic Load
(complexity
of new
information)

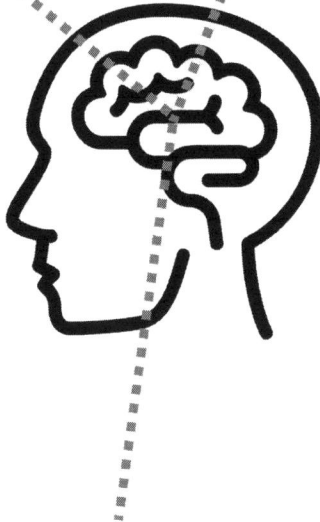

Extraneous Load
(unnecessary and
distracting info)

Three types of cognitive load

IX

Final Word

50

Remember

Classroom management is straightforward but not easy. Keep working as mastering the few principles in this book, keep testing, and you'll soon master the art and science of classroom management. If you'd like to read more about any of the topics here, please visit my website (see below). You can also search through the bibliography / notes section.

I hope you've found some useful ideas from reading this book (if you have found it useful, please leave me a short review on Amazon– thank you, you're amazing!). I wish you well in implementing these ideas, and good luck on your teaching journey!

Visit my Website

I write somewhat regularly at www.barefootTEFLteacher.com so I hope you'll join me there to read and comment.

Sign Up to My Newsletter

You can find a sign-up box on my website. I send a newsletter every week, where I share ideas and updates from the world of language teaching.

Find Me on Twitter

I go by @BarefootTEFL and I tweet language teaching and learning news and interesting articles I come across.

Email Me

What did you think? Let me know at david@barefootteflteacher.com - I read every email and do my best to respond.

Notes

INTRODUCTION

1   Weller, David. *Lesson Planning for Language Teachers: Evidence-Based Techniques for Busy Teachers.* UK: Stone Arrow Publishing, 2019.

WHAT IT'S NOT

2   Hz, Aseele. 'Hedonic Adaptation', 16 August 2020. Researchgate

AIMS

3   Evertson, Carolyn M., and Carol Simon Weinstein, eds. *Handbook of Classroom Management: Research, Practice, and Contemporary Issues.* Mahwah, N.J: Lawrence Erlbaum Associates, 2006.

BENEFITS

4   Daniels, M. L. (2009) 'The Three Fs of Classroom Management', *AASA Journal of Scholarship & Practice*, 6(3), pp. 18–24.

5   Marzano, R. J., Marzano, J. S. and Pickering, D. (2003) *Classroom management that works: research-based strategies for every teacher.* Alexandria, VA: Association for Supervision and Curriculum Development.

DECISIONS

6   "No plan survives contact with the enemy" a variant of a saying from: https://en.wikiquote.org/wiki/Helmuth_von_Moltke_the_Elder

A POSITIVE ENVIRONMENT

7   Weinstein, Carol S. 'The Physical Environment of the School: A Review of the Research'. *Review of Educational Research* 49, no. 4 (1979): 577–610. https://doi.org/10.2307/1169986.

8   Doyle, Walter. 'Ecological Approaches to Classroom Management'. In *Handbook of Classroom Management: Research, Practice, and Contemporary Issues*, 97–125. Mahwah, NJ, US: Lawrence Erlbaum Associates Publishers, 2006.

9   Barrett, P. S., F. Davies, Y. Zhang, and L. Barrett. 'The Impact of Classroom Design on Pupils' Learning: Final Results of a Holistic, Multi-Level Analysis'. *Building and Environment* 89 (July 2015): 118–33. https://doi.org/10.1016/j.buildenv.2015.02.013.

DECORATION

10   Hanley, M. *et al.* (2017) 'Classroom displays-Attraction or distraction? Evidence of impact on attention and learning from children with and without autism', *Developmental Psychology*, 53(7), pp. 1265–1275. doi: 10.1037/dev0000271.

11   Thomson, P., Hall, C. and Russell, L. (2007) 'If these walls could speak: reading displays of primary children's work', *Ethnography and Education*, 2(3), pp. 381–400. doi: 10.1080/17457 820701547450.

12   Cullingford, C. (1978) 'Wall displays-children's reactions', *Education 3-13*, 6(2), pp. 12–14. doi: 10.1080/03004277808558889.

13   Hanley, M. *et al.* (2017) 'Classroom displays-Attraction or distraction? Evidence of impact on attention and learning from children with and without autism', *Developmental Psychology*, 53(7), pp. 1265–1275. doi: 10.1037/dev0000271.

LAYOUTS

14   Doyle, W. (2006) 'Ecological Approaches to Classroom Management', in *Handbook of classroom management: Research, practice, and contemporary issues.* Mahwah, NJ, US: Lawrence Erlbaum Associates Publishers, pp. 97–125.

15   Adams, R. S. (1969) 'LOCATION AS A FEATURE OF INSTRUCTIONAL INTERACTION', *Merrill-Palmer Quarterly of Behavior and Development*, 15(4), pp. 309–321.

16   Evertson, C. M. and Emmer, E. T. (2013) *Classroom management for elementary teachers.* 9th ed. Boston: Pearson.

SILENCE VS NOISE

17   Rowe, M. B. (1986) 'Wait Time: Slowing Down May Be A Way of Speeding Up!', *Journal of Teacher Education*, 37(1), pp. 43–50. doi: 10.1177/002248718603700110.

18   Stahl, R. J. (1994) *Using 'Think-Time' and 'Wait-Time' Skillfully in the Classroom.* ERIC Clearinghouse for Social Studies/Social Science Education Bloomington IN. Available at: https://www.ericdigests.org/1995-1/think.htm (Accessed: 14 February 2021).

AWARENESS

19   Kounin, J. (1970) *Discipline and Group Management in Classrooms.* New York: Holt,Rinehart & Winston of Canada Ltd.

20   Emmer, E. T. and Gerwels, M. C. (2006) 'Classroom management in middle and high school classrooms', *Handbook of classroom management: Research, practice, and contemporary issues*, pp. 407–437.

OVERLAPPING

21   Rogers, R., M., S. (1995) 'The costs of a predictable switch between simple cognitive tasks.', *Journal of Experimental Psychology: General*, (124), pp. 207–231.

22   Kounin, J. (1970) *Discipline and Group Management in Classrooms.* New York: Holt,Rinehart & Winston of Canada Ltd.

STUDENT-TEACHER RAPPORT

23 Newman, R. (2000) 'Social Influences on the Development of Children's Adaptive Help Seeking: The Role of Parents, Teachers, and Peers', *Developmental Review*, 20, pp. 350–404. doi: 10.1006/drev.1999.0502.

DIFFERENTIATION

24 Tomlinson, C. A. and Eidson, C. C. (2003) *Differentiation in practice: a resource guide for differentiating curriculum, grades K-5.* Alexandria, Va: Association for Supervision and Curriculum Development.

25 Anderson, L. W. (2014) *A taxonomy for learning, teaching, and assessing: a revision of Bloom's.* Pearson new international edition. Harlow: Pearson Education.

SCAFFOLDING

26 Bransford, J., National Research Council (U.S.) and National Research Council (U.S.) (eds) (2000) *How people learn: brain, mind, experience, and school.* Expanded ed. Washington, D.C: National Academy Press.

27 Vygotskij, L. S. and Cole, M. (1981) *Mind in society: the development of higher psychological processes.* Nachdr. Cambridge, Mass.: Harvard Univ. Press.

28 Berk, L. E. and Winsler, A. (1995) *Scaffolding children's learning: Vygotsky and early childhood education.* Washington: National Association for the Education of Young Children (NAEYC research into practice series, v. 7).

EXPECTATIONS & RULES

29 Rosenthal, R. and Jacobson, L. (1992) *Pygmalion in the classroom: teacher expectation and pupils' intellectual development.* Newly expanded ed. New York: Irvington Publishers.

PREVENTING MISBEHAVIOUR

30 Doyle, W. (2006) 'Ecological Approaches to Classroom Management', in *Handbook of classroom management: Research, practice, and contemporary issues.* Mahwah, NJ, US: Lawrence Erlbaum Associates Publishers, pp. 97–125.

SERIOUS MISBEHAVIOUR

31 Anderson, M. (2015) *The first six weeks of school.*

TEACHING VS LEARNING

32 Willingham, D. T. (2009) *Why don't students like school? a cognitive scientist answers questions about how the mind works and what it means for the classroom.* 1st ed. San Francisco, CA: Jossey-Bass.

THINKING ROUTINES

33

COGNITIVE LOAD

34 Sweller, J. (1988) 'Cognitive load during problem solving: Effects on learning', *Cognitive Science*, 12(2), pp. 257–285. doi: 10.1016/0364-0213(88)90023-7.

35 Mayer, R. E. (2002) 'Cognitive Theory and the Design of Multimedia Instruction: An Example of the Two-Way Street Between Cognition and Instruction', *New Directions for Teaching and Learning*, 2002(89), pp. 55–71. doi: https://doi.org/10.1002/tl.47.

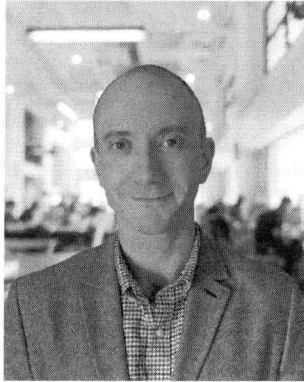

About the Author

I'm David Weller – a teacher, trainer and insatiable coffee drinker. I started teaching in 2003, and since then I've been a taught, trained, examined, managed, just about everything else it's possible to do in the education sector.

The best way to keep in touch is to subscribe to my monthly newsletter. It's totally free, and I don't pass on your details (so no spam, ever). If you have any comments, questions or suggestions, I'd enjoy hearing from you.

Thanks for reading, and the best of luck with your teaching journey!

You can connect with me on:
- https://www.barefootteflteacher.com
- https://twitter.com/BarefootTEFL
- https://facebook.com/barefootTEFLHQ

Subscribe to my newsletter:
- https://www.barefootteflteacher.com/newsletter

Also by David Weller

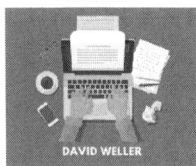

Lesson Planning for Language Teachers

Do you want to plan better, faster, and worry-free?

Most of the time, planning sucks. It takes *ages*, and your next lesson is in 20 minutes.

You **CAN** finish your planning faster, with awesome lesson activities, and still have time to chat in the staffroom. Find out how.

Essential Classroom Management

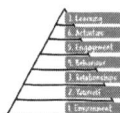

Transform your teaching with a new seven-step classroom management system that's the key to a calm class, relaxed mind, and classroom full of learning!

Printed in Great Britain
by Amazon